Communicating Strategy

...so it is compelling, people get it, and execute it.

Reviews for *Communicating Strategy*

'*Everything in this book is obvious* – after you have read it. *It is a practical book you can use and apply every day, as well as being a guide to planning a larger communication strategy.*'

Martin Coombes, Partner, Innovation llp

'*The messages in this book are important for anyone interested in strategy! Phil Jones discusses the critical issue of communicating strategy – and what's best – he communicates his messages in a very engaging and easy to understand manner.*'

Bernard Marr, Chief Executive, The Advanced Performance Institute

'*Communicating Strategy communicates well – in direct and accessible language. Phil articulates a route to success by both building on the strengths of relationships at work and by demonstrating how to deal with the disconnect that can occur in leading change when strategy is not jointly owned. Phil's research has evidently been done and applied to his conclusions. Above all, it is apparent that he has walked the approach he advocates...well communicated.*'

Shelagh Grant, Chief Executive, The Housing Forum

'*Phil Jones gives practical skills for bridging the gap from mission, to transmission, of strategies for change in organizations. He draws comparisons with different models of change and gleans some "differences that make a difference". One of the ideas that make this book stand out is how it challenges some basic assumptions about change and more importantly about people. It is after all people who have to initiate, manage and embody or incorporate transformation and transition, if people do not feel safe, then it is unlikely that they will respond well to uncertainty.*

Though the busting of myths in management is a key component of the book, I feel more left with the idea that tasks get completed, or not, through relationship: that trust and generative collaboration are vessels that hold the possibility for success.

Having a background in the discipline of Neuro Linguistic Programming I appreciated the use of some of the technology, concepts and models throughout the book. As Neuro Linguistics is a technology which is used for building models of success, it is a well done application of the ideas.'

Judith DeLozier, NLP University[1]

'*No worse that any other management book you have made me read.*'

Deborah Jones, The author's wife

---

1   Judith has been a trainer, co-developer, and designer of training programs in the field of Neuro-Linguistic Programming since 1975. A member of Grinder and Bandler's original group of students, Judith has made fundamental contributions to the development of numerous NLP models and processes. Judith is a co-developer of a number of projects applying Systemic NLP, ranging from modeling leadership, to health care and cross-cultural competence. She is presently an associate of NLP University.

Communicating Strategy

PHIL JONES

GOWER

Published by
Gower Publishing Limited
Gower House
Croft Road
Aldershot
Hampshire
GU11 3HR
England

Gower Publishing Company
Suite 420
101 Cherry Street
Burlington
VT 05401-4405
USA

British Library Cataloguing in Publication Data
Jones, Phil
  Communicating strategy
  1. Communication in management 2. Strategic planning
  3. Leadership 4. Employee motivation
  I. Title
  658.4'5

  ISBN-13: 9780566088100

Library of Congress Control Number: 2007931873

Printed and bound in Great Britain by TJ International Ltd, Padstow, Cornwall.

Contents

List of Figures

List of Tables

Preface

In early 2006, I noticed that my websites were getting a lot of activity on the topic of 'communicating strategy'. It was closely behind 'strategy' as a topic of interest. As I researched the Internet to see what else was available on the topic, I realized it was a topic that was not well covered.

However, within a few sites I came across one that suggested five principles of communicating strategy, of which one was, 'You should not communicate your strategy, as you will leak your strategy to the competition.' I was incensed by this idea, for two reasons. If your strategy is so unsustainable that your competitors can simply copy it that easily, then it is a pretty poor strategy. Secondly, if you don't tell your people about your strategy, how can they possibly execute it and help you refine it and deliver it?

So, incensed by the 'don't communicate your strategy' idea I looked for books on communicating strategy. There seemed to be none. There were plenty on strategy formulation, and strategy implementation. There were many on public relations. There were lots and lots of interpersonal communications. But there seemed to be nothing specifically on communicating strategy. So I decided to write one.

I have been helping organizations describe, develop, articulate and communicate their strategy more effectively for over 12 years. I have been privileged to work in some great consultancies with some great colleagues and wonderful clients. The experiences that make up this book come from a whole variety of different types of organizations. I have been on the receiving end of strategy, as a line manager, and helped to formulate it in a variety of organizations. When I worked for the originators of the balanced scorecard, Norton & Kaplan, the emphasis was always on the understanding and drivers of the strategy much more than just its measurement and management. Rather it has been about helping the management team be clear about the underlying thinking around the strategy, so they could walk out of their boardroom with a complete and consistent understanding in their heads of what they were trying to achieve, and why. Much of this has involved helping them have a richer conversation as they develop and articulate it. They then have a deeper understanding of the assumptions and underlying thinking, so they can tell the story effectively to their people. The techniques I have seen, learnt and developed through these experiences are in this book.

This book started as a short e-book, but soon developed into this fuller book. Its working title was 'Heads, hearts and hands', which reflected the strategy being in the head, as a logically correct thing to do; being in the heart, as an emotional response and engagement; and being in the hands, so it is executed.

Part of the reason for the growth in the content was the need to explain the many practical ways in which the strategy is communicated. It is easy to say what should be done. It takes longer to explain how to do it, and I wanted the 'how to do it' in this book. I also wanted to provide people with options. There is no one way to communicate strategy well. This is a book of strategy communication tactics that people can pick and choose from as they see fit.

My work with clients has often involved coaching them in language and presentation techniques to help get the message across. Many of these techniques I have learnt in my training as a facilitator and presenter. Some come from my training as a Neuro-Linguistic Programming (NLP) master practitioner. However, I rarely tell my clients that they are using NLP techniques, preferring just to show people great ways to do things. Of course if they ask, I tell them (and I have had several side conversations that go, 'You are using NLP techniques, aren't you?'). You will recognize techniques from a variety of sources. No prior understanding of these techniques or approaches is required for this book.

I recently bumped into a chief executive I had worked with around 3 years earlier. She said that one of the biggest differences the work had made was to the middle managers, who were now engaged with the bigger picture. They were no longer working in silos, but making a much larger contribution to the organization. I like to think that this has not only helped the senior managers, but has made the working lives of those middle managers better, as well as those of the organization's customers.

Throughout this book there are many examples that illustrate points or provide an example. They have come from my many clients over the years and some I have interviewed for research. It is in the nature of strategy work that it remains confidential. They know who they are. There are many others, such as fellow consultants and colleagues, who have also contributed to this work in so many ways that they are probably not aware of.

I am grateful to my colleague Liz Morrison, who read an early draft and encouraged me to develop the book properly. Also to Jonathan Norman of Gower, who saw the value of such a title and on reading a version kindly referred to it as 'a lovely little book'. Gower has moved away from their normal practice and are publishing this as a paperback rather than a hardback. I thank him for his support.

Finally I would like to thank my wife Deborah, who read through the various versions, tidying up my language, checking for errors and correcting my grammar. Any remaining errors are mine. The final recommendation comes from her, when she said, 'This is no worse that any other management book I have read.'

Phil Jones
Excitant Ltd
www.communicating-strategy.com

1 They Don't Get the Strategy

These were precisely the words the chief executive used, 'They don't get the strategy.' This was not a small company: it was listed on the FTSE100. It was not a particularly new strategy, as they had been implementing it for around 2 years. It wasn't a particularly new management team, and the chief executive had been in post around 4 years. It was a well researched and documented strategy. It was so well documented that it took me a week to go through all the strategy documents I had been given as background reading.

Yet the chief executive was still frustrated. As far as he was concerned, 'They didn't get the strategy.' If they don't get it, then it is unlikely to be implemented or deliver the results. He was right to be frustrated.

He is not alone and the problem is not peculiar to his type of organization. I have heard this complaint, in all sorts of organizations from large commercial, to public sector bodies, from medium-sized listed companies, to family and privately-owned organizations. Despite all the valiant efforts of the management team, the message is not getting through as intended by the person who conceived it.

Yet some organizations communicate their strategy really well. They manage to communicate what they want to achieve and how they will go about it. They get people motivated and remove the blocks that have prevented the strategy from working in the past; blocks that may be deeply embedded within the culture of the organization. They get people behind the strategy, adding to it and making it work in their part of the business. In short, they make it happen.

This book is about what you can do to make the difference in communicating your strategy. It provides you with the tools you can use to plan how the strategy will be communicated. It presents techniques to help communicate the strategy. It equips you with ways to think about how strategy is communicated, analyze what might have gone wrong in the past and make decisions about the best way to get your strategy across. There are some techniques you will be able to apply immediately and others you can incorporate into your communication plans.

ONLY FIVE PER CENT UNDERSTAND THE STRATEGY

Some research was conducted into why many strategies seem well conceived but poorly executed.[1] It concluded that whilst many organizations have some success with their strategy, almost nine out of ten organizations failed to *fully* implement their strategy as they had planned. The first figure in this research suggested that, of all the staff in the organizations involved, only 5 per cent of them understood the strategy. A different and more recent survey suggested that this figure was around 8 per cent. I suspect the difference is not significant.

This limited understanding of strategy amongst its staff is an important issue for an organization. Even if the figures were out by a factor of ten, that means only half know what you are trying to achieve. If only one person in 20 understands your strategy (and presumably that one is executing the strategy) what opportunity are you missing with the other 19? It also raises the question, 'Whose strategies are the other 19 executing?'

It is not just a question of communication. It is also a question of trust. In a 2005 survey of 1 100 employees by Mercer Human Resource Consulting in the UK, just 36 per cent of workers trusted management 'to always communicate honestly'. A similar survey of 800 US employees found that 40 per cent of respondents felt the same.[2]

I suspect these figures also reflect different populations within the organization, and would vary with different levels of management and employee. Nonetheless, if you truly believe that your employees are a critical asset and fundamental to your success, can you afford to have so few of them trusting, understanding and helping you to implement your strategy?

HEADS, HEARTS AND HANDS

Lots of time is spent developing a strategy and planning its implementation. Yet a simple fact remains: no matter how good the thinking behind the strategy, it is a waste of time if it is not in the heads, hearts and hands of the people who need to execute it. Of course, it is helpful to have it available for reference on the shelf or in the computer, and to keep the auditors happy. If that is where it stays, it is a waste of paper, and it has been a waste of management time and effort.

---

1   This survey was conducted by Renaissance Worldwide in 1996. The other three main issues that prevented strategy being executed were: a lack of alignment in the organisation to support the strategy, the misalignment of incentives and the lack of time executives spent discussing strategy.
2   CFO Europe, Edward Teach, Suspicious Minds, June 2006, www.cfoeurope.com/displayStory. cfm/7013332.

This book is about communicating that strategy, getting that engagement and getting feedback from it. As you read through this book and think about the questions it raises, the suggestions it makes and the examples it uses, you will see how it is designed to help you get the strategy into the heads of your people and develop that engagement.

The book is designed to help you build skills, think through the issues and develop a plan for communicating your strategy. Of course, that plan should be in your head, which is why it is not formalized until the end of the book. By the time you reach it you will have developed lots of ideas and have started putting them into action.

A wide range of experiences in a wide variety of sizes and types of organization has gone into this book. These organizations range from large commercial and multinational companies to small family-run businesses, from large public sector bodies to city councils, from dot.coms, through traditional manufacturing companies to pure service organizations. You can apply the ideas and experience in this book to them all.

At a minimum, the strategy must address the simple logic of, 'Where are we going and how are we going to get there?' It will engage the heads of your staff. But that is not enough. It is also about getting to the hearts of your people. Whilst the cold logic of *Star Trek*'s Mr Spock is useful, it is the emotional commitment and engagement that often makes the biggest difference. The passion with which people engage customers or commit to activities makes a massive difference to people's productivity and results. It also makes a big difference to how people feel about being at work and how the organization's community and society plays in their lives. This passion and commitment will come from the passion and commitment you have when you communicate the strategy.

It is also about getting it into the hands of people, so actions are taken. Many strategies have had compelling logic and been passionately delivered, but have still failed in their execution. Sometimes the organization itself acts to stop change happening. Sometimes people need a compelling wake-up call. Sometimes, people simply need to know that they have permission to act differently and no longer be constrained by the rules that bound them. So, whilst this book is about communicating your strategy in an organization, it is applicable to communicating all sorts of changes in an organization, its culture and its values.

THE APPROACH AND STRUCTURE OF THIS BOOK

Many books suggest what you should do to solve various problems. They focus on what to do and how to do it. My experience is that such advice is often limited in its usefulness. It is not just doing things that matters; it is how you think about what you do and what you believe about what you do. These often have a far greater influence on success.

This book aims to give you tools to make decisions for yourself. It does not try to say, 'If you do all these things, you will successfully communicate your strategy.' What it sets out to give you is the underlying thinking, tools and techniques that you can choose from. More importantly, it provides advice on when to use those tools and how best to use them.

It is said that bad workers blame their tools. Likewise, an unthinking manager uses tools just because they are there. That is the route to fad management. Please do not go down this route.

This book aims to help you develop the thinking behind good communication of strategy. It aims to help you develop your judgement as to how best to communicate in a particular situation.

How you communicate your strategy will depend upon your personality, your thinking styles and your motivations. One purpose of this book, particularly in chapters two and three, is to help you to realize the impact of your way of thinking and your preferences. This does not just apply to individuals. Organizations, too, have personalities, thinking styles and motivations. These personal and organizational preferences will also influence how you will tend to prefer to communicate your strategy. This clash of preferences between individuals or between individuals and the organizational character often lies at the root of poor communication. Understanding it will help you address it, before you make mistakes.

Chapter 2 will confront some heresies about communicating strategy; who to tell the strategy to; and how people will react, benefit and be involved in the communication. The purpose of this chapter is to open up your thinking around communicating strategy. You are not expected to believe all these heresies immediately. You are only asked to start to question your own thinking and beliefs around communicating strategy. This chapter is also intended to make you think about who you should include in your communication and why you should engage them.

'I WAS IN A WARM BED, THEN I WOKE UP IN A PLAN'

This is a line in a Woody Allan movie.[3] If the strategy is communicated badly or implemented badly, it is how it can feel to many people.

Having spent a long time developing the strategy, you will be in a different place from those not involved. Just think: you may have spent several months

---

3   From the film *Shadows and Fog*, 1992, MGM, directed by Woody Allen.

of detailed work analyzing the problems, gathering facts, exploring ideas and developing the solution. Your head has moved on from where you were several months ago. However, others have not been involved. They may know something is going on, but will not know what it is. Part of the challenge you face is to get yourself back to the situation where you started and look at where you are now, as if you were still there.

Throughout this book you will be asked to consider the situation and look at the strategy from the perspective of others. This is a skill that some people take time to build. It is one thing to say, 'I would not do that in their shoes.' You are not them. You are not in their shoes. There is a Native American saying, 'Judge not someone until you have walked a mile in their shoes.'

To walk in their shoes, you have to ask the question, 'How would I think if I were them?' Alternatively, ask, 'What would I have to know or believe to act like that?' Chapters 3, 4 and 5 will help you develop these skills and, through these, a more effective communication style.

5

Chapter 3 will help you identify the various players[4] that you will be dealing with, the reactions you want from them, the quality of relations you have and the timing of the communication. This will help you explore with whom you should communicate, why and how. By the end of this chapter you will have built up a picture of your players and how you could communicate with them. You will have started to assess the quality of the communication channels that are also in use.

If strategy is about change, and measured by results, strategic communication is measured by changes in actions and behaviours. Chapter 4 explores how change occurs. It describes the mindsets, motivations and typical reactions that you get when new strategies and change programmes are announced. Much of this book is about making sure the strategy is communicated so people understand and are engaged with it. However, there is also an aspect to communication that is no nonsense discipline. At some point, when people are not complying, you will have to get serious and potentially get rid of people. This chapter also explores some of the aspects of communication that go behind the message to show you are serious. This is, 'The discipline of change'.

Chapter 5 considers 'What is in it for me?' from the perspective of the various players. You can explore 'What's in it for them?' from different people's perspectives so you can build an even richer understanding of the various players involved.

4	This sentence uses the more general term 'players' to represent the many people affected by the strategy, rather than the more specific and overused expression 'stakeholders'. For the sake of simplicity, I have primarily used 'stakeholders' throughout the rest of the book, even though the stake in many cases is somewhat tenuous. They often seem more of an interested party or player in the organization's strategy.

THE STORY OF THE STRATEGY

The book contains many small case studies, anecdotes and stories. These all come from real organizations or clients and are designed to illustrate points, bring out aspects of the technique or give you an example of how someone else has tackled a situation. This theme of telling stories permeates the book. Part of the art of communicating your strategy is telling its story. Storytelling is an art that transcends cultures. Chapter 6 explains how to develop the story of your strategy so it is complete. Chapter 7 provides techniques to tell the story more effectively.

Chapter 6 concentrates on *the content* of the story of the strategy. What is the strategy and what are the aspects of it that will need to be told? How can we tell these various aspects in a coherent way? The quality of the thinking within the strategy will strongly influence the telling of it.

Chapter 7 addresses *the telling* of the story of the strategy. It explores ways in which you can get your message across more effectively; how to engage people, pacing them and communicating the message, so it engages the many different ways in which people think about things. It also provides ways to prevent you stifling feedback through the accidental messages you might send out. It tells you how to be more systematic about gathering feedback and getting people to participate in the strategy, because listening sensitively to this feedback enables you to refine the message and its communication.

ORGANIZATIONAL AND PERSONAL CONGRUENCE

When we listen to presenters or politicians, we instinctively notice how congruent they are. We may think, 'That person is lying or does not believe what they have just said.' In some cases they may say one thing at one time and something different at another time. In some cases what they say may not align with what they do. Chapters 8 and 9 address this question of congruence, not just for individuals but for the management team and the whole organization.

What applies to individuals also applies to the whole management team. If the management team leave the boardroom with different stories, then it will quickly become apparent to the rest of the organization. So Chapter 8 describes what can go wrong and helps you address the congruence of the management team before the message gets out. That way the message is consistent and aligned.

This congruence also applies to the whole organization. This is not just about the people telling the story. Are you about to communicate a strategy, only to be undermined by the very organization in which it will operate? In 'The handcuffed organization', Chapter 9 provides ways you can check the coherence and integrity of the whole of the organization's message. It provides a checklist of organizational processes, systems and cultural components that you can use to ensure the message is not undermined.

Finally, Chapter 10 will bring all these pieces together by providing a plan for developing your communication strategy and a contents list for that communication strategy document.

WHAT DO WE MEAN BY STRATEGY, ANYWAY?

This book is about two aspects of strategy: 'What is our organization's strategy?' and 'What is our strategy to communicate the organization's strategy?'

This book refers to 'the organization's strategy', without limiting what you may mean by it. In common with most strategy writers, the word will be used in a variety of ways through the book. This looseness can create problems of understanding – strategy is an overused word. It is useful to be clear precisely what is meant; for example:

> *'You can strategically add strategy to any strategic sentence, to give it any strategic meaning you strategically want it to strategically have.'*

Unfortunately this almost random dropping of the word 'strategy' into sentences is all too common. In many instances, simply using the word 'important' would be sufficient. Yet we like 'strategy' because it sounds more 'strategic' (important). Every alliance and partnership is a strategic alliance or strategic partnership. Every important customer seems to be a strategic one. Where are the tactical ones? Every communication is strategic. Where are the tactical messages? Every investment is a strategic investment. Where are the tactical ones?

There are many uses of the word 'strategic' that are assumed or hidden when the word is over used. I suggest that, when you hear the word, you think to yourself which version is meant. Here are just a few uses, with examples of how they are used and what they really mean:

- Strategy as important: 'I want this (or me) to sound more strategic (important) than it really is.'

- Strategy as a plan: 'This is our strategy (plan) for improving the business.'

- Strategy as a position: 'How are we (positioned) strategically in the market?'.

- Strategy as differentiation: 'What is our strategy (what is our unique selling point or differentiation)?'.

- Strategy as a wider perspective: 'Be more strategic (stand back from the problem or take a helicopter view).'

- Strategy as purpose: 'This is our strategy (purpose).' 'What are we trying to achieve strategically)?' Often used in contrast to the actions (tactics) to get there.

- Strategy as a long term view: 'Think more strategically (think longer term).'

- Strategy as a response: 'What is our strategy (what is our response to our competitor's actions)?' Both chess and price wars provide examples.

- Strategy as choice: 'What we choose to do, and choose not to do.'

- Strategy as politics: 'He is very strategic (he plays politics well).'

- Strategy as a pattern of behaviour: 'What is our strategy (what has been our persistent pattern of behaviour in this situation)?'

This last one is extremely useful. If ever you are unsure about the strategy of an organization in the past, it is useful to ask the question, 'What has been the persistent pattern of behaviour, over the past few years, that has brought you here?' The answer will reveal the actual strategy in use, rather than the one they say they have.[5]

Ultimately it can be useful to ban the word 'strategy'. Doing so forces people to say what they really mean. It will expose those who drop strategically into sentences just to sound important. It will help those who are discussing different aspects of strategy to be far clearer about what they mean (be it plan, position, purpose or response), making it easier for others to understand and contribute as well.

Whatever form your strategy takes, or meaning it has, this book provides you with tools to articulate and communicate that strategy, so people get it. Just be clear what form of strategy you are communicating and how you are using the word.

CONCLUSION

By reading this book, doing the exercises and trying out these ideas, you will improve your ability to plan your organization's communication of its strategy and communicate your strategy better. You should also improve your judgement about communicating strategy, so you can make your own decisions about what is right in each circumstance.

---

5   'Thinking strategically; talking strategically', by Phil Jones provides a more detailed and extensive description of these uses of the word 'strategy'.

The nature of a book is that it tends to be read from front to back. Do not let this stop you going straight to sections as you feel they would be useful for you.

As you read through, there are plenty of examples to think about. You may find they ring true for you or remind you of situations you have had in the past. I encourage you to pause and think about the lessons these experiences have provided.

There are also questions in each section. I encourage you to do these as you go through and not to skip them. Thinking through them, in the order they have been presented, is a valuable way to ensure that you are getting the most from this book and will apply the lessons it contains to your situation. Of course they also act as a checklist you can come back to when you are using the techniques in your organization.

2 Ten Heresies

This chapter asks, 'What do you believe about communicating strategy?' It will help you understand what *you* believe about this process. It is important to realize what *you* believe about the people with whom you will be communicating. This understanding will help you avoid pitfalls and open your eyes to opportunities that you and others may be missing.

We will explore two of the biggest crimes in the communication of strategy: underestimating your people and failing to get your strategy out to your people. Research suggests that only around 5 to 8 per cent of the people in an organisation understand the strategy.[1] Even if this statistic is out by a factor of ten, at least half do not understand, and are not available to assist with, support, inform or execute, the strategy. Why does this happen? Why is this figure so small?

This chapter addresses some of the underlying reasons for this low figure. The reasons are expressed as 'heresies', for they are not common thinking. The heresies are designed to get you to think about the assumptions that you make. You may disagree with them. You may start to challenge some of the underlying beliefs you may have about people and the value of communicating with them. You don't have to change your beliefs when confronted with something that contradicts them. However, just try these new beliefs on for a while. See how it feels to believe them. It is a route to some fascinating insights. I invite you to do that in this chapter, and in the book as a whole.

OK, brace yourselves! I am about to commit some heresies. Some people will not like me saying these things, but try them out. They provide some useful insights and you will easily bring to mind examples of where you have seen these in action.

- Heresy number 1: People are not stupid.

---

1   In-house research conducted by Renaissance Worldwide Ltd (1998), 'Barriers to strategy implementation', and others since.

- Heresy number 2: You don't have all the answers.

- Heresy number 3: Your staff are interested in the strategy.

- Heresy number 4: People can be trusted.

- Heresy number 5: People respect it, if you assume they are intelligent.

- Heresy number 6: You are always communicating, even if you think you aren't.

- Heresy number 7: You don't have to communicate with everyone.

- Heresy number 8: The rumour mill communicates faster than you do.

- Heresy number 9: Strategy does not exist in plans.

- Heresy number 10: People like change.

HERESY 1: PEOPLE ARE NOT STUPID

I occasionally meet people who say, 'That person is really stupid.' Every time I do, I wonder to myself which one of them is actually being more 'stupid'.

Everyone is basically rational. The catch is that what they believe to be true is not the same as what I believe. That does not make them stupid. They just believe something different from me. Just because I cannot explain their actions does not make them irrational or stupid.

To understand things from their perspective you need to get into the position where you think as they do. A powerful way to do this is to ask, 'What needs to be true for me to act as they do in that situation?' This is called 'second positioning'.

This question provides powerful insights into where apparently irrational behaviour is coming from. When you see something that looks 'irrational' or 'stupid', ask the question, 'What would have to be true for me to do the same thing?' You won't necessarily get the answer that drives that person, but it will give you insights to think about.

The person labelling the other as 'stupid' is the one with the limiting belief. They are deciding it is not worth even trying to understand where the other person is coming from.

They believe that it is not worth trying to understand where the other person is coming from, and what they might believe, as it would only be irrational anyway.

Many years ago I used to run what I nicknamed my 'plonker' strategy. It worked very well. I would quickly suss out who were 'plonkers' and not bother with them. I would concentrate on the other people.

When I first realized this might be a limitation, I thought I should make an effort, so I broke the habit of a lifetime and got chatting to one of these 'plonkers'. He was really interesting and I learnt a lot from listening to him. I realized how silly and restrictive my strategy had been. By eliminating all these people, I was missing out on insights and ideas that were really valuable.

Now I run the opposite strategy. Those I used to class as 'plonkers', I now call 'interesting'. I now seek out those I used to ignore and, guess what, they are always interesting and often insightful.

Questions

Who do you currently regard as 'stupid'? Be honest now.

Who are you ignoring in your strategy who actually might be insightful or interesting?

What are you going to do about it?

What might they believe, to do what they do and behave like they do?

HERESY 2: YOU DON'T HAVE ALL THE ANSWERS

One misconception about management is thinking you have to have all the answers. Let's take an extreme example. Have you ever met a manager who gets involved in every decision that is made? You may know one, have worked for one, or be one.

A chief executive was extremely frazzled, stressed and overworked. He told me he wanted to be more strategic, and, at the same time he was telling me that he was not happy 'leaving things to other people'. They could not be trusted; they made silly decisions and mistakes. Oh, and he wanted to stop his chief operating officer from also getting lost in too much detail. He wanted to make sure all the decisions were made properly. The problem was people could not be trusted to do things properly.

Just for a moment, imagine having to make every single decision. Every single decision is brought to you, so you have to make it. Everyone who works for you has been trained to bring decisions to you, so you will make them.

Imagine the information and detail you would have to have in your head: production schedules, plans, customer information, product knowledge and so on. Imagine the responsibility. It is mind-boggling.

Now, imagine what it is like for the people who 'work' for you. You will have trained them not to make decisions, but to procrastinate until they get your approval. This is not managing, let alone leading: it is doing.

Part of management's function is to develop people, so they understand their roles and responsibilities, and what they are trying to achieve. The point of employing people is so they do things, rather than you, so you get the best from them. It is the same with knowledge. You shouldn't try to know everything. You shouldn't need to.

It is important to be grounded: to know what is going on and how things work. Of course, it is management's responsibility to lead. Of course, it is management's responsibility to think further out, to think the unthinkable, to consider the risks.

On the other hand, you are employing people who are intelligent people. I have been in plenty of situations where I have been 'managing' and 'responsible for' people who had far more skills, knowledge and experience than I had. I was managing projects with extremely technical people and teams with experienced customer sales people. Management is about getting the best from these people, not doing it for them. Leadership is about creating the space for them to succeed.

When you talk about the strategy, you will be talking to people who know the customers extremely well. Perhaps they have worked with, or for, competitors. They will have the skills and training that you will not have. They may have information that you do not have. They will certainly know the processes better than you, so they can contribute ideas, explanations, questions and objections.

These are really valuable. Don't overlook them.

Questions

Who should you trust that you currently don't?

Who are the really valuable people in your company with insights?

Who might have insights that you do not have from the top?

Who, perhaps by sharing some knowledge with them, might be a valuable source for you?

Who can you involve who would have some answers to the uncertainties you have?

HERESY 3: PEOPLE ARE INTERESTED

Whenever I talk about communicating the strategy, at least one person in the room responds by saying, 'My staff are not interested in the strategy.' This shocks me. These people believe that their staff just want to come work, do the job, get paid and go home at the end of the day.

There was an advert on television where headless bodies march off to work and sit in front of computers. This raises two concerns: that the manager has already decided that these people are not interested, and that the people involved have no choice. As a consequence, you have a group of people who are not engaged or do not care about the organization.

The strategy may not mean that these people's jobs will become redundant (I bet they would be interested then). It may mean a change in what they do. Moreover, they are being denied the chance to take an interest.

Sometimes, they have been trained not to care. Communications may have been so poor in the past that they have switched off. Getting it right, by following these guidelines, could well engage them (but you might have to work hard).

If we could take the view that they do care, surprising things may happen.

> *The strategy of a large oil company was being rolled out to tanker drivers. The objective of the session was to give them some 'personal scorecards' with five or six personal measures and objectives. One view was that they only needed to see what concerned them. However, it was decided to show them the bigger picture.*
>
> *As this was being explained, one raised his hand. 'Are you saying you want competitor information?' 'We do', was the reply. 'Well, we spend hours a week in cafes talking with other drivers about their trucks, their reliability and fuels. We can gather information about what they are using and how reliable they are. Would you like information about what oils they are using and how they are perceived and performing? We can get it in tanker loads for you. Would that be of interest?'*
>
> *'You bet!' was the reply.*

The lesson here is that people are interested. Often they have been ignored, or excluded, and not engaged.

Questions

Do you have managers who believe their staff do not need to know the strategy?

Do you have any groups that have been treated like this in the past and now need extra special care and attention?

What have you done over the years to switch people off from the strategy?

Which groups appear uninterested?

How might it be helpful if you involved them?

HERESY 4: YOU CAN TRUST PEOPLE

There is a deeper malaise than this. If you search the web for information about communicating your strategy, you may come across 'advice' on communicating strategy that says, 'Don't tell people. It will only leak to your competitors.' I find this really scary, for several reasons:

1.   If you don't tell them, then what strategy will they be following?

2.   Your competitors will find out soon enough. Also, if you have a strategy that is so unsustainable that it is sunk as soon as your competitors find out, then it is probably not a strategy worth having.

3.   Most strategies are based on the competencies, knowledge and skills of the people in the organization. If you don't tell them what you want, how will they know to develop their skills and know their value?

4.   Are you really saying that you don't trust your staff? What sort of culture have you created?

I have met enough senior people over the years who have admitted (in closed surroundings) to having moles in their competitors' organizations. This is a separate issue; one that needs tackling specifically. You need to keep confidential information away from competitors. You need to protect yourself against industrial espionage, but it is one thing making sure your competitors don't know what's going on and quite another not letting your own people know, or trusting them.

This approach also leads to the 'terrorist cell' approach to communicating strategy. That is, tell people only what they need to know, and make sure they know nothing about the other parts of the picture. Of course the catch is then that the 'cells' can't communicate, cooperate and work together: probably the exact opposite of what you want to achieve.

Not trusting people will generate people you can't trust. There is a vicious circle for you.

Questions

Are there any groups of people to whom you may have sent a signal of lack of trust in the past?

Who are they?

How do you know?

What could you do to fix the situation?

How will you demonstrate trust to your people this time?

HERESY 5: PEOPLE ARE SMART

Some communication panders to the lowest common denominator. The story is told in such a simple way because, 'They would not get it otherwise.' There is an assumption about the intelligence, or interest, or capability of your people that drags everyone down to the lowest point.

The opposite is true. People are remarkably clever and smart. If you have any doubts that people are smart, just ask what they do outside work. You will be surprised what they achieve, organize and contribute. They will work things out and fill in the gaps if you do not provide them. Unless you fill those gaps, they will do it for you – with what they want to fit in it.

Assuming people are not interested or can't contribute is terrifically patronizing and a great missed opportunity. Yet if you were to ask your staff what they do and what responsibilities they take on outside work, you might be surprised. Try it.

'Talking down' sends out a signal to people that is like the, 'We don't trust you' statement, except it is more subtle. It says, 'We don't respect you,' or 'We think you are not very smart' – neither of which you want to happen, do you?

It is sensible to explain the strategy in pieces and in different ways. Repeat the message and have pieces that are remembered for the information and detail they contain, not for the hidden message within the message.

Question

What have you got to gain from explaining the bigger picture?

HERESY 6: YOU ARE ALWAYS COMMUNICATING

Here is the irony: You cannot not communicate. Even if you think you are not communicating, you are communicating.

By not saying things, you still are sending messages. (Just look at some couples you can think of. They may not say anything to each other, but are saying everything at the same time.)

Try it! Next time you are with someone, try not speaking. See how long it is before someone asks you what is wrong and starts guessing what the issue is. Sometimes they will assume there is something wrong with you. Sometimes they will assume it is something wrong with them. Sometimes both.

By 'not communicating' the strategy you are sending a message. During the development of the strategy you may be busy for long periods in closed rooms, or on away days. You may be involved with external consultants. You might simply be resolving disagreements as to the best way to proceed. During this time, you are probably not communicating.

This space is not really a space. Everything you do and say is communicating in one way or another. You may not say anything, but people spot body language, longer nights, closed doors, meetings with different people, talking with different suppliers, changes to scheduled meetings. People will fill in the message during this period, as they want to. Some call this hallucination. Some simply say it is reading their own interpretation into things. Your lack of communication may be interpreted as:

- there is a major change coming;
- we don't want to involve you;
- this is hard work;
- we value consultants over our own staff;
- you will have to manage on your own and make decisions for yourselves while I am away;
- here they go again. Let's just get on with stuff.

However, in other organizations it may be interpreted as:

- she is protecting us from the corporate problems, so we can get on with things;
- they will tell us soon enough;
- they don't want to bother us, as we have enough on our plates.

Most of these are, of course, interpretations, hallucinations or people jumping to conclusions. They are filling in the space with their own interpretations. The interpretation will depend upon the climate and culture of the organization and the history of communication. If there has been a history of poorly implemented change, these might be the signs of the next wave. If there is a new person in charge, people will be looking for signs of their style. If there is a culture of trust, people are willing to wait to see what comes out.

Questions

What messages have you been communicating?

What messages might people have being reading into your actions?

Is that consistent with what you want to communicate?

HERESY 7: YOU CAN OVER COMMUNICATE

Some say, 'Communicate, communicate and communicate!' However, the expression says everything and nothing at the same time. It emphasizes communication, however, it says nothing about how, why, when, to whom, or even when to stop.

It can also be taken too far. This whole book is about communicating more content, better, to more people, through more channels, consistently, effectively and with integrity and congruence and listening to the feedback. You can communicate too much of it with too many people; saying too much, meeting too often, 'just for the sake of it', and saying too little.

You can communicate with too many people. There comes a point when you are talking to too wide an audience. Large briefings have one person talking and several hundred listening. They are effective to get a message across, but if ten people ask questions, you can bet that by question number six, the other 399 people are itching to leave.

You can say too much. It may be inappropriate to provide a detailed competitor analysis to all your staff. A succinct summary to key people may be enough to get the message across about the threat. In contrast, providing legitimate competitor information to sales staff can be very valuable. Being better armed, they are able to convert objections into a sale.

Have you had the 'yet another strategy meeting' syndrome or the 'here is another boring briefing' meeting? You go to meetings for the sake of it. The value they add is diminishing. If you have nothing new or interesting to say, don't waste people's time. Convene a short meeting, say there is nothing new, let people raise any questions or issues and then get on with things. This is far better than holding meetings on a fixed agenda without a real reason.

It also has the advantage of providing an opportunity to pick things up. Whilst you might not have anything to say, there might be questions or feedback from the floor that are important to other people in attendance. The boy who cried wolf pretended there were wolves around so that when they actually appeared, the cries were not believed; if you avoid pointless meetings, when you do have something important to say, it will not be ignored, lost in the background noise or treated as just another example of meeting for the sake of it.

Beware of cancelling meetings because you are too busy. This can be just as frustrating. Other people have made space in their diaries and you have abused it.

Questions

How has your communication been received today?

What has been the effect of this?

What might you need to be careful of in this communication of the strategy?

HERESY 8: THE RUMOUR MILL COMMUNICATES FASTER THAN YOU DO

Ever thought of asking, 'What rumours have we heard?'

In one organization where I worked, it was the regular question at the end of management meetings. At first I thought it was just my manager collecting intelligence and asking a smart question in our team meetings.

After a few meetings, with different managers, I realized it was a standard question in several different meetings. Key managers were sniffing out the rumour mill to see what was floating around. It wasn't all managers – that would have been too blatant. It was those with a good wide network.

Then the penny dropped. Senior management were deliberately setting off rumours and seeing what came back. How they came back and the distortions within them gave clues as to what people were thinking. It was also a way of priming the message.

I like the idea of asking, 'What rumours have we heard?' Don't start rumours, but it is an informative question to ask, even if you are not starting them. It means you can stop the inappropriate rumours at source and notice what might be leaking. There is no smoke without fire.

In contrast, there is the whole area of psy-ops (psychological warfare). They say, 'The right bullet can stop a person; the right weapon can stop a regiment; the right message can stop a war'.

Questions

What rumours are circulating in your organization?

How do you pick up the rumours that are circulating around the organization?

How could you tap into the rumour mill?

Who are the key players in accurate rumours? For inaccurate rumours?

Where do these rumours originate?

HERESY 9: STRATEGY DOES NOT EXIST IN PLANS

When you ask for the strategy, you are often given the plans. Usually these are paper documents. In one place I was provided with a beautifully bound set of folders in a box that measured a foot square. In other organizations you have to find the person who can explain it to you. I strongly recommend that all plans should be burnt.[2]

The reason is simple. Strategy happens and is implemented on a day-to-day basis all over the organization. When people are taking decisions, they are implementing the strategy. As they do this, they are not constantly referring to the thick paper-based copies of the plans: they are using what is in their heads. If the plans and strategies are in their heads, then they are executing the strategy. The plans can safely be burnt, as they have served their purpose.

Of course, if your plans are not in their heads, then they are either implementing their own strategy or someone else's. In either case, whatever plans you had are a waste of time and they might as well be burnt. Consequently, 'All plans should be burnt.' This belief represents an underlying theme of this book.

If you are reading this book you probably already realize that strategy does not exist in plans. The whole point of this book is that you do not 'just give them the plans'. Consider what you can do instead. The approaches outlined in this book help you to tell the story, and tell it well, with conviction and passion. You can get the underlying thinking into people's heads.

This only demonstrates that the importance of the strategy planning process is not to produce plans. It is the planning process that is important. It develops an understanding amongst the management team of why the strategy exists and what it is about. The process of planning and the understanding that comes from it are more important than the plans themselves.

The challenge is how to communicate this understanding of why we are doing this and what we are doing.

Questions

What strategy is in people's heads at the moment?

In whose heads is your strategy? In whose heads is your plan?

Does the plan explain how you got there and why the strategy exists?

Do you understand the assumptions and limitations and know how to spot them?

---

2   Of course auditors get really upset when you suggest this. Try it – it is great fun.

HERESY 10: PEOPLE ACTUALLY LIKE CHANGE

There is a cliché that amazes me every time I hear it. It presumes so much about people. I believe it is fundamentally incorrect.

'People do not like change.'

The phrase is almost a cliché. Yet eliminate all change, and you have sensory deprivation. Sensory deprivation is where people are put in an unchanging environment of white noise whilst floating in water. It is probably the least changing environment I can think of. It is regarded as a form of torture.

Why do people say they don't like change? Have they had poor experiences of being changed? It is not change that people don't like. Almost everyone I know likes to improve. If you take the word 'change' in the sentence above and replace it with the word 'improve', you get a completely different sense and meaning. That is a way to reframe 'change'.

The word 'change' carries no implication of improvement or things worsening. It is neutral in that respect.

The real issue is often about how the change is carried out. It is not having control over change that affects people. It is not being consulted. It is not being able to understand why the change is occurring. It is not being able to influence these changes or the rate of change. It is badly implemented change that people do not like. Can you blame them? They would not like badly implemented improvements.

It also presumes people are all the same. We like some stability. There are people, like me, who like change as well. I get interested when projects are a challenge and bored easily when projects are stable and under control. Many entrepreneurs like the variety and challenge of building a new business. When it becomes stable, they get bored and it is time for them to move on.

Strategy is about change. Do not assume that all change will be resisted and that people will see it as bad. If you implement it well, people will like the changes and wonder why you did not ask for them earlier.

Questions

What do you believe about change, for yourself?

What do you believe about change, for others?

Are the changes you are making improvements? Improvements for the company?

Improvements for the people involved?

What change needs to occur for your strategy to work?

CONCLUSION

In this chapter, we have confronted some heresies head on. I don't expect you to just roll over and accept these as true yet. Some you may agree with. Some may be deeply embedded beliefs for you. You probably disagree with me on at least a few of them. I hope so anyway. The purpose of this chapter is to open up your thinking.

In summary, people are not stupid. They can be trusted, they are intelligent and, if you try to have all the answers, you will fail. If you respect people and communicate that respect, they will give you respect.

You are always communicating, whether or not you think you are. People will fill in the gaps for themselves. The rumour mill is particularly good at this, so stay in touch with it.

Strategy is about change and improvement. Don't assume people don't like change and improvement. It is poorly implemented improvement they don't like. The strategy will only be successful if you get it deeply into people's heads. That is what the rest of this book is about.

3 Communicate What, to Whom and Why?

In the previous chapter, we opened your mind to the range of people and the effects of communication. In subsequent chapters we will cover what the message in the strategy is and how to get it across. In this chapter, however, we will look at whom you might wish to communicate with, why you are communicating with them and what sort of response you are looking for. By the end of this chapter, you should have a clear view and feel for:

- To which people do you need to communicate the strategy?

- Why are you are communicating to them?

- How do you get the timing of the communication right?

- What routes do you have to those people at the moment? How effective are they?

- What responses would you like to get, or expect, from them?

We will provide some tools, yet also warn you against over analyzing these 'stakeholders'.

This chapter will help you understand the quality of communication that is going on at the moment. It provides a basis for the later chapters, which will consider their thinking more deeply. Having worked through this chapter and the subsequent ones on telling the story of the strategy, return to this chapter and review the questions again. By thinking through the strategy as we describe it, it will assist you in thinking through who to communicate and how.

WHICH PEOPLE DO YOU NEED TO COMMUNICATE TO?

The very first question to ask is actually a double question: 'With whom do I want to communicate, and why?'

While working with a management team on their strategy, a key aspect of which was influencing managers in other associated organizations, we had identified the need to get the message out and also learn from their issues and pressures as well. 'No problem', they said, and showed me their communication plan.

Whilst it was heavy and thick (and signed off) one thing struck me immediately. I was looking for the list of people they had to communicate with. I could not find it. So, then I looked for what they were trying to achieve with their communication and the key messages they were trying to get out. I couldn't find that either.

What I did find was a lot of explanation of what they currently communicated and how they communicated. They held meetings, used a newspaper, issued brochures, and carried out staff briefings. It documented what they did.

When asked who were the really important people they needed to be talking to and influencing, the people they listed were not in the plan. All they had done was to document the existing channels, rather than the important targets and the message. They had looked at what they had, not what they wanted.

Stakeholder list

The first step is, 'With whom should we communicate?' If you have a clear view of who needs to be communicated with, and why, you have a great starting point. To develop a stakeholder list we ask the question, 'With whom should I be communicating?'

Examples could include:

- your workforce – but this might be broken down by:
    - different sites
    - different front line departments
    - different support departments
    - different layers of management
    - different players in management and the organization
    - different countries or regions
    - those directly affected who need to change
    - those indirectly affected
    - those who work with those who are affected
    - unions or worker representative groups.

Externally it may include:

- customers
    - large ones

- – smaller ones
- – buyers
- – users
- – their customers
- – distributors, retailers and agents
- suppliers
  - – sales and key account managers
  - – delivery people
- partners and alliances
  - – strategic partners and alliances
  - – tactical partners and alliances
- investors
  - – large shareholders
  - – smaller shareholders
  - – angel investors
  - – banks and other lenders
- government agencies
  - – central government agencies
  - – local government agencies
- regulators in regulated industries
- media
  - – national papers
  - – local papers
  - – trade news

Question

To which groups or types of people do you need to communicate the strategy? Complete this list before you go further.

This is called a target stakeholder list. Obviously you can develop this into a table with groups of people, names, what you want and how to communicate to them.

Now you have this list, you can look at the relationship between and amongst them.

Stakeholder relationships and diagrams

Once you have a list it is worth developing a 'stakeholder diagram'.[1] A stakeholder diagram allows you to show the main groups of players and stakeholders with whom you want to communicate, what they influence, how well you connect with them at the moment and their relative importance. The value is that it quickly shows the whole of the community you are dealing with, in a single diagram. It also helps to explain the communication strategy as well.

You can draw these in a number of ways. I prefer a particular style that shows the relationships and importance of the various players and stakeholders.

As you can see from the example (Figure 3.1), there are often a collection of different stakeholders. Notice how they are groups that cluster together. These are groups that have close relationships amongst themselves.

Notice how some stakeholders are positioned farther away from the centre, whilst others are nearer. This is not a geographic distance. This represents the effort that it will take to get the message out. It represents the distance between the stakeholders in the relationship.

Some groups are accessed through other groups. This is a clue that you will not only have to brief the people in the group, but equip them with communication tools. Also note that they are different sizes, representing their importance or the size of the community.

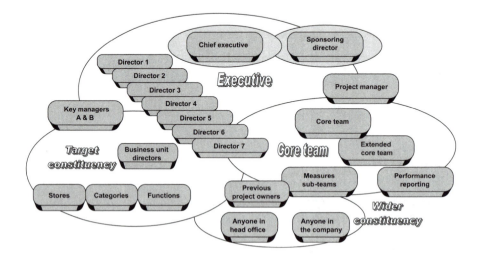

Figure 3.1   Stakeholder diagram

---

1   Often called a player diagram.

Questions

Draft your stakeholder diagram. What insights is this giving you?

As you work through this book, be sure to revise it.

Some people start with a sheet of A3 and put all the groups on sticky notes. Others go directly into PowerPoint. Whichever you prefer, expect to refine it as your understanding progresses. If you are finding it hard, it may be a sign that you are unsure of your stakeholders. In which case, ask yourself the question, 'Who could help you develop this list?'

Having developed the stakeholder view, it is now worth asking, 'What are the real relationships?'

The real relationships

Most organizations have a formal organizational structure chart. These represent the hierarchy of responsibility. Communication rarely follows these lines. There are lots of informal networks and relationships that actually lubricate the organization and make it work.

Key people are actually the network hubs. They are the well-connected people who know a lot of people and through whom a lot of the communication goes.

One way to understand the communication channels in an organization is to analyze the flows through these key players. List the top players in a circle and assess the communications that flow between them (see Figure 3.2).

You will see that there are some people with whom many others communicate and to whom many of the lines go. There will be others with smaller networks. Those people with many connections are usually well known in the organization. They are the well-connected influencers in the organization: excellent networkers, whose contacts extend well beyond the organizational chart and often well beyond the organization. They will frequently be people with a wide network across the industry.

Another way to describe these people is 'Mavens' (Gladwell, 2002).[2] These people are:

- well-connected;

- knowledgeable on subjects and also what people can do for other people;

- have a reputation for reliability and trust.

---

2   Gladwell, M. (2002), *The Tipping Point: How Little Things Can Make a Big Difference* (London: Abacus). The expression 'Maven' was popularized in this book.

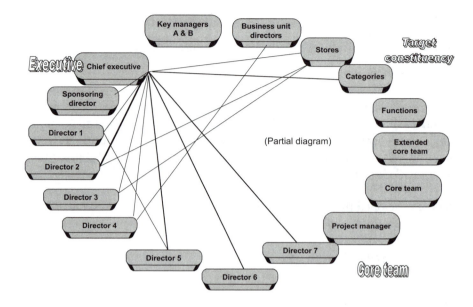

Figure 3.2   Relationship and communication mapping

When creating your stakeholder list and diagram, it is worth identifying individuals who are highly connected and key influencers. Remember, when doing this sort of analysis, it is no respecter of grade. It is not about how highly paid people are, or the size of their office. It is about the quality of their network and relationships and the degree of trust they have. There are tools that analyze e-mail traffic to create these pictures, but these omit the relationships that happen face-to-face and over the phone.

Also, highly connected people know other highly connected people. That is the crux of the tipping point model. A tipping point occurs in a market when highly trusted and well-connected people start using and recommending a product. These have a disproportional effect on the reputation and interest in the product and so the chain of events occurs such that the product becomes popular.

It is the same with knowledge. Trusted sources pass messages on. Moreover, they pass reliable messages to people who believe it and therefore are comfortable passing that message on to others.

Questions

Who are the highly connected people in your organization?

Who are the highly influential people?

What are their networks?

Where are they on your stakeholder analysis?

How well plugged into them are you?

How could you plug into them?

Highly influential people don't have contacts in the tens or hundreds. They have them in the thousands, and the quality of their contacts and connections is far higher.

A word of warning: these 'Mavens' have a reputation built upon the quality of their information, as well as the quality of their network. Therefore, they will not spread unreliable information, nor be seen to act in an untrustworthy way. Their reputation is too valuable for that.

So, you cannot exploit them. They will act as a conduit if it is in their interests, rather than yours. If it enhances their reputations, or helps their networks, they will support it. If it seems it will harm their reputation and networks, they will not support it.

WHAT REACTION OR RESPONSE DO YOU WANT?

Having listed the stakeholder groups, the next question is, 'Why am I trying to communicate with these people?' Put simply, 'What do I want to achieve?'

This is simply *your* purpose in the communication. This is important because it explains why *you* believe it is important that these people understand the strategy.

The emphasis is important. When people do this analysis, they tend to think about what reaction they want people to have. I normally suggest people do this the first time through, so they get a clear view of their own thinking and what reaction they want or expect.

Think through this question *as if you were someone in that group*. Ask, 'If I were a member of that group, what would I think of the communication?' This forces you to imagine being in that group receiving the message, rather than simply telling them. It also helps you to think through the strategy from *their* perspective rather than yours.

For instance, if you are communicating to investors, think as if you were an investor. 'What would I want to know?' 'Why is it important to me?' 'How does this compare with other communications and strategies in the same industry?' 'What else have I heard recently?' 'What else am I used to hearing about?' 'What methods of communication do I like?' 'What do I want to hear, even though I won't necessarily like the message?' 'What must I hear?'

Questions

Desire:

'What reaction do you want these people to have?'

'What actions do you want these people to take?'

From their perspective:

'What do I think of the communication?'

'What do I want from this communication?'

Expectation:

'What reactions do I expect them to have?'

'What actions do I expect them to take?'

These questions can have quite different answers. These are really important questions. Often it is not about telling them; it is the response you desire. What do you expect? What would you like them to have?

The important thing in each case is to think through the situation from their perspective:

1. What response do you want them to have?

2. What message is important for them?

3. How could you get to them?

There are some situations where you will not be able to reconcile these desires. The reaction you want and the reaction you get won't match. Also, what you want and what you expect can also be two different things.

> *In the UK, in 2006, the French owners of the Peugeot car plant at Ryton, in Coventry, announced its closure. The unions and workers were 'up in arms'. Some wanted to know why they were not warned. However, the owners decided they could not have let slip beforehand that such a closure was imminent.*

> *At the same time, there were various studies going around the company that the Ryton plant was the least efficient. Obviously, this could have been an incentive to managers to make it more productive. At the same time it was a plant originally built nearly 50 years ago and long overdue for reinvestment.*

> *The union reaction was to petition the French management not to close the plant. Obviously going on strike was not a good idea at this stage. All that would do is save the company money, confirm the commitment to close the plant and ensure the workers were not paid from now as opposed to being made redundant in 12 months time.*

There was a large amount of media coverage. Whether this was first initiated by the French management, the local management or the unions and workers is unclear.

The closures did not affect the French plants. This led to some suggestions that inefficient French plants were being saved by sacrificing the British plants.[3]

The important thing is to be conscious that these tensions exist. That way you can explain why you were unable to communicate them beforehand.

CHANNELS AND THEIR EFFECTIVENESS

At the start of this chapter we had the example of an organization that created a communication strategy by documenting the communications channels it currently had. In contrast, we have concentrated on:

- Who is important in this strategy?

- What response do you want?

- What do they need to know?

- What are the real connections?

- When do they need to know?

How do we get to these people? What channels exist already and how effective they are? The purpose of your communication channels is to get to as many of your targets, as reliably and quickly as possible and get maximum feedback. So in choosing the channels, there are six main criteria. These are:

1. Does it provide feedback or is it one way?

2. Is it reliable? Can I control the message that passes through it?

3. Can I communicate a rich message or only a simple one?

4. Will it go to many people or only a few (broadcast or narrowcast)? Will it be a personal or an impersonal message?

5. How long does it take to prepare?

6. How long does it take to communicate, once it is ready?

The channels split into three main groups. Face-to-face communication channels rely on a personal contact. They include individual meetings, team meetings, large gatherings and conferences, as well as the informal networks.

---

3   For more details of this story see the BBC article '2,300 jobs to go in Peugeot closure', 18 April 2006, <http://news.bbc.co.uk/1/hi/england/coventry_warwickshire/4919312.stm>.

Electronic channels provide a powerful way to get a message out quickly. They include email, phone, messaging, blogging, message boards and discussion forums. In general these are less personal than face-to-face contact, but provide an effective way to get a message out quickly and sometimes reliably, though often with less feedback.

More traditional channels, such as newspapers, notice boards and letters home are still used. They can be slower and less reliable, but provide a useful reinforcement of the messages sent down other channels.

When considering which channels, or combination of channels, to use you should consider the characteristics of each route. The best route may be a combination of channels that mix face-to-face communication, electronic channels and other, more traditional approaches. Appendix A lists these channels and describes the advantages and disadvantages of the various types of channel. The appendix covers:

- Broadcasting or narrowcasting: Is this good for getting a message out to a large body of people, or better for a more personal, one-to-one, communication?

- Feedback: Does the channel provide a mechanism for obtain feedback? Is it a one-way or two-way communication? What is the quality of the feedback?

- Reliability: How reliable is this as a channel to get a message out? How sure can you be that the message will be received and understood?

- Ability to get a rich message across: Some channels are limited in their ability to get words, pictures and emotions across. Others are far better at getting a rich and complicated message across.

- Time to prepare: How long does it take to prepare a message for this channel?

- Speed of communication: Once out, how long does it take to get the message to all the intended recipients?

Questions

For each group, think through:

1. *What channels of communication do you already have open with these people?*

2. *Who owns them? Who controls them?*

3. *Do they communicate well?*

4. *Are they available at the right time, or are they better used to reinforce the message and therefore you will need a specific way to get to these people in the first place?*

5. *How are they regarded? Are they respected? Are they believed? Are they timely?*

6. *Do they work? Can they still work?*

7. *Do they provide feedback? If so, how well, and how quickly?*

As you list the communication channels you have to each of the groups you have identified you will find that some of these will be formal and others informal. Some will be regular and others ad hoc. For instance, the company newspaper is probably monthly, but distinctly one-way. Whilst you may have formal union meetings monthly, you have enough trust and the opportunity to chat with the union representatives outside those meetings. The briefing in the canteen might be ad hoc, but provides little opportunity for interaction and feedback. There may be a hundred people there, but only a few (the brave or the rebellious) will be vocal. That is not quality feedback.

Once you have a starting list, give every channel a mark out of ten for its suitability. The mere act of trying to score them will force you to think about them.

Questions

How does this channel score out of ten?

How well do I understand this channel?

What is good about it?

Does it provide effective and timely feedback?

What do I need to improve to make it a ten?

Table 3.1 provides an example of what this might look like.

Who owns these channels?

It is OK to rely on a channel if you own it and have some control over it, or you can trust it. If you haven't, then it may not be a reliable channel. The irony is that the channels you don't own are often the most influential. The challenge is to exploit the influential channels, and show integrity along the ones you control. It is about the quality of the message and the integrity of the messenger, as much as the channel.

Whilst you might own the company paper, the formal briefings and the company meetings, each has its disadvantages. The company newspaper is very one way. Formal briefings are useful for telling, but less effective at getting rich feedback, as we have discussed.

One of the interesting effects of the Internet is that the channel of communication is no longer owned by the organization. It is a channel

Table 3.1   Example of an analysis of communication channels

Group	Channels	Score /10	What works? What does not?	Improvements?
Executive team	Board papers	4	Formal presentations. Not very timely. Need to get on agenda. Slow to get information to them. Requires long time to prepare.	Agree regular reporting timetable for programme. Get our board team sponsor to brief as well.
	Individual briefings	8	Good for individual comments and feedback. Hard to get to people regularly. Won't get to whole team consistently.	Agree timetable with key people.
	Through their managers	7	Good contacts with some of the executive team. We need better contact with finance and marketing directors.	Find ways to engage the finance director and marketing director.
	email	5	Some read – others filtered by their PAs.	Needs focused information for them as well as overall project briefing.
	On demand	6	Do they have the project team members contact details? Can they access the website? Is this convenient?	Let them know when important stuff happens. Use RSS[1] feed to notify them of changes.

1   RSS provides an automatic feed from websites when the content is updated.

owned by the people who use it. There are plenty of examples where the Internet has opened up communication and let through what people really believe. In other cases where censorship has occurred, people have stopped using the channel and its value has been lost.

Questions

Who has control of the channels you have identified?

Can you rely on them?

What credibility do they have?

Equality of access to channels

Whichever channel of communication you choose, be careful to ensure equality of access for people who may have visual or hearing impediments or have other access constraints. Not everyone will be able to access the channels as easily as others. If you send everything out by electronic post, or blog, and have not provided a way for your visually impaired staff to access them easily, you are potentially excluding them and discriminating against them.

Take advice on which are the best channels and how to serve them, though be careful to ensure the advice is good and that you follow it.

> *Whilst implementing a change programme in a city council, we were conducting training sessions for all the key managers. We had a couple of blind people in the sessions and realized the PowerPoint presentation would not help them. So, we were advised to type up all the notes and get them converted to Braille using the council's Braille service.*
>
> *You would think that the Council's Braille service knew what to do. However, it produced a massive pack of continuous Braille with none of the structure, section markers, slide numbers or pointers for the start of any section on it. It was so badly produced that the people was completely unable to follow the Braille copy.*
>
> *We were embarrassed and horrified. It was completely inappropriate and the whole pack had to be redone.*

The lesson is, beware. Find out what works and what does not. Speak to people about their particular needs. Ensure that the services you use know what they are doing and work for the people with whom you are trying to communicate.

QUALITY OF RELATIONSHIPS

Once you have a view of the groups, it is useful to review the quality of relationships.

It may be difficult from within corporate communications or a strategic planning group to get an objective assessment of this, so get out and talk to people in these areas.

This is not about the channels of communication, but can often be about the organizational structure, geography or roles themselves.

> *In a large financial institution, one particular group had a distinct culture. Whilst most of the staff dealt with life assurance, a small team of 20 dealt with investment and stock market savings products. This group was positioned amongst the other groups in an open plan office and, at first glance, you would not notice the difference.*
>
> *However, their statutory requirements demanded a strict timescale with the deals closed for the day promptly at 4 p.m. The manager ran a tight ship and had a well-established team. They had their own systems. They were very focused on service standards and customer relations; something with which other parts of the business had been struggling.*

Thus, there was a unique sub-culture within this group. Some 10 years later, the organization was bought out and broken up. This particular group remained intact and was sold off as a separate entity.

Despite being colocated, it had its own particular role and culture.

The quality of the relationship is about how close people are and how trusted the network is. The reasons for this can vary enormously.

Five years after a merger of two financial institutions, there were still people saying, 'He is from organization A, whilst she is from organization B.' There never really had been a merging of the two organizational cultures. Whilst there had been some redundancies, the merger had been a case of, 'This manager and his team can take over this role, whilst this manager and her team can take over that role.'

So, there were still cultural boundaries and an undercurrent of 'them and us'. It was subtle, but still there. Some people bore their differences long and deep.

There are lots of examples where the quality of relationships with different groups will vary. Even different offices on the same business park can create divisions, let alone separating departments by town or even countries.

The wonders of the telephone, Internet and video conference are no substitute for face-to-face relationships.

Yet, if there are groups within your target audience who have historically had poorer relationships with either the centre or other parts, then these need addressing.

Questions

What is the quality of the relationships within and between the various groups you have identified?

Do some groups demand special attention?

Do some groups have a reputation for poorer relationships?

Is this something that the strategy is explicitly addressing?

TIMING

Having considered with whom you need to communicate and the channels you have available, you should also consider the timing. Do you want to get the message out to these people early, or should you hold back until you are ready? Clearly, the choice will depend upon the stakeholder and their influence, power and role in the change, as well as your intentions towards them.

Holding back

As the Peugeot Ryton plant example above showed, timing is a key element of the communication approach.

> *Prior to the announcements, the workers were clearly unaware. You can imagine in this situation that the unions were unaware, but perhaps were first to be told, with very quick follow-ups to the workers within the same day.*

> *Whilst the workers were unaware, it would have been necessary for some of the Ryton management to know precisely what was going on, so they could plan their actions and think through the responses.*

So, there is a phasing of the communication of the roll-out. The question is who needs to know, by when?

> *A large insurance company with a large sales force was about to substantially revise its working practices, means of remuneration and cost base. The sales force accounted for two-thirds of costs when commission was taken into account. Commission was a huge influence of sales force behaviour.*

> *A director was appointed to lead the project team, review the options and plan the changes. The IT department was outside this team. When they heard about the project, and knowing that they would have substantial and radical changes to make, they approached the project to see how they could help.*

> *They were told it was 'top secret'. Nothing could be passed to them and they would not be trusted as they were concerned the changes in commission, structure, remuneration and working arrangements would leak out to the workforce before they wanted them to know.*

> *IT realized that their track record with 'legacy systems' was that they typically needed some 9 months for major changes. The timing of the project meant they would have 2 to 3 months: a seemingly impossible timescale. Moreover, the changes were going to be radical and enormously wide ranging (the old sales force structure had been effectively hard coded into most of the main administration systems).*

> *IT came up with an original solution. It created a list of possible options and asked the director in charge to tell them what was a waste of their time. In effect, 'Tell us what we should not spend our time on.'*

> *This gave them the chance to assess what were the more likely options and develop some alternatives. By doing this, they were able to work around the very fixed systems that they had.*

> *In the end, IT were officially given 8 weeks' notice of the actual remuneration arrangements which, together with their preparatory thinking and work, they were able to deliver on time. This was the fastest they had ever delivered a major and fundamental change in the core systems.*

This example is interesting on many levels. It particularly highlights the issue of timing. Who should know what, by when? It also highlights that what was an acceptable notice period for the project was (normally) completely unacceptable for the IT people.

It also raises a large question about trust. What was it about the history of the relationships between IT and that director or the project team that stopped them trusting IT with the knowledge they needed? Conspiracy theorists might suggest IT were being set up to fail. The end result was that IT was seen as delivering exceptional responsiveness. In reality, there were very few people in IT who needed to know and therefore needed to be trusted. There was a history of poor relationships between some people in IT and that particular director. On the other hand, one could argue that the IT service needed to be far more responsive, and this forced their thinking and approach to be more innovative and different.

Whichever is the case, this example highlights how the timing of the roll-out of a strategy can depend on a variety of components coming together. There was no way the new structure could have been rolled out without the new remuneration system in place.

So, the timing of the roll-out of the information can be driven by the design of the strategy and the implementation components. Some departments such as IT, marketing and HR may need to know about the forthcoming changes before others, to help or avoid being a constraint. In other strategies, the same departments may lead the way.

Questions

Look again at your player list and diagram.

Given the timing of the roll-out, who needs to know what, and by when?

What are the critical dependencies?

Who are your trusted contacts?

Is there anyone you are excluding for historic reasons? Is that still valid?

Surprise, surprise!

The lessons in this book will sometimes appear contradictory: deliberately so. Having just described the need to hold back, there may be others groups to whom you have to give some advance warning. These might be the few people of greatest influence or those who need preparation time to plan for the forthcoming changes.

One of the first lessons I learnt in consultancy was 'no surprises'. The client should not be surprised when they see the results of the analysis and the recommendations. We sat down with them and explained where we were coming from before handing over the final report. This allowed us to do two things:

1. ensure the client was briefed on our findings and get his or her reaction;

2. ensure we had not made any glaring errors or omissions.

The same applies when telling the strategy. There are ways to test the reaction to the story and of the audience.

Your stakeholder analysis provides a valuable insight into where you might test your strategy. You will want to choose trusted sources.

CONCLUSION

This chapter has been about preparing the ground. By thinking through with whom you want to communicate, what message you want to get across, which channels are available and how you might use them, you are preparing the way for the message.

Beware of starting when you are not quite ready. Starting when you are unsure of your strategy, story or message will create quite the wrong impression. There is a difference between not being ready and giving people advance warning. If you are doing the main communication, rush it and do it badly, then a large part of your credibility will be blown.

In contrast, there is value, when the ship is sinking, in warning people to get ready to get off. Alternatively you might want to try out some ideas on the workforce. Perhaps you are changing shift patterns to accommodate fluctuating markets, and you have seven options. How do you choose? You could set up a workers' forum elected from the shop floor, or use the existing one if you have it in place. You can bounce ideas off the smaller group, filter them down and then have them make a decision, or offer the final two options to the rest by a ballot.

The main group might complain they were not consulted. At that point you can remind them that they elected the group precisely for that purpose. You can take on constructive ideas, but quite often you may find these comments are simply, 'We wanted to know sooner,' and the simple answer is, 'For confidentiality reasons we chose not to.'

This approach can also be used with trusted managers. Using key players and influencers in the organization (and outside) as bouncing boards can help to settle down the options and gauge reaction, prior to rolling out the message to a larger audience.

You can spend far too long preparing the delivery of the message. By the time you get around to telling people, they have worked it out for themselves (or decided it is too late).

Questions

What parts of your message need testing and refining?

Who are your key influencers?

Are you willing to trust them for the benefit of getting a better answer or a more effective message?

The central message of this chapter is preparation and planning. Think through to whom you are communicating, and why. What communications have they received so far and what might they be expecting? It has also been about the channels that exist today. Some are formal and in your control, but perhaps the most powerful are the informal ones.

Having been through the questions and developed a stakeholder chart with communication channels, it is time to think through the motivations of the people involved, which is the subject of the next chapter.

4 Understanding and Motivating Change

When you are communicating strategy, you are communicating change. Otherwise why are you communicating it? If strategy is about creating and making change happen, communicating strategy is about communicating that change and helping to bring it about.

To succeed you can no longer have the organization performing, operating or behaving as it does at the moment. You may have decided where you are and where you want to take the organization, but you have yet to convince the rest of the organization of the same thing. So this chapter explores the mindset that people may be in and what influences them.

Heresy number 10 (Chapter 2) was that people do like change. Yet we hear so often that people do not like change. I believe people do like change. What they do not like is having no influence over the changes that are happening to them. The phrase is a criticism of how change is carried out. Challenge those people who use the phrase, 'People do not like change,' so they start to think differently.

This chapter provides an overview of some of the models of change. It starts by exploring some of the theoretical models of change, and moves onto some practical actions that are often taken in the early stages of communication.

The theoretical models describe the way people change and the stages they are seen to go through. It then describes three common drivers that are used to instigate and influence change. These drivers of change need to account for how people are thinking.

The practical models include some common techniques that are used to communicate the need for change. You have to be seen to be serious about change, especially when past behaviour becomes unacceptable. The softer aspects of making change happen often need to be accompanied by a large stick, so the discipline of change is also explored.

The chapter concludes with seven-step model of change, derived from this thinking and experience. Almost all change and communication programmes go through similar stages to succeed.

STAGES OF CHANGE

Several models of change describe the stages that people go through when change occurs. These are useful for tracking the progress of change, but do not help explain how to bring change about. Three of these are:

- unfreeze, change and re-freeze;

- commitment, enrolment and compliance;

- the Satir family therapy model of change.

Unfreeze, change and re-freeze

An often used metaphor for change is, 'unfreeze, change, re-freeze'.[1] This suggests that, for change to occur, people have to 'unfreeze' from their current state, go through a change of some kind, and then 're-freeze' into the new shape. It is as if they were water in an ice-making mould.

This model suggests that there are three stages to think about when planning a change. First, how will you 'warm up' the organization to prepare for change? Second, how will you now alter the organization, so that the new changes are in place? And finally, how will you 're-freeze' it so that the new practices and beliefs are embodied in the organization and remain in operation?

Whilst this describes what some people are doing, it does assume that people are 'frozen' in the first place, that they need 'unfreezing' in some way, and that 'unfreezing' needs to occur before the change can take place. It also suggests that they need to be 're-frozen' at the end.

These are useful assumptions, but they may not always apply, as we shall see later. It is useful to compare this metaphor of ice with one of modelling clay, which is malleable all the time. Is this metaphor of ice more useful in understanding what you have to do than a metaphor that uses modelling clay or malleable clay? Some people use the expression, 'They are putty in my hands,' which suggests a similar image.

Questions

Do you have an organization that is fixed and frozen or malleable?

Does it need unfreezing or is it ready for change?

---

1   Lewin, K. (1951), in D. Cartwright (ed.), *Field Theory in Social Science: Selected Theoretical Papers* (New York: Harper & Row).

Commitment, enrolment and compliance

Another variation of this is 'commitment, enrolment, compliance'.[2] This is similar to the 'freeze' example, but is more useful because it describes a response that people will have that demonstrates that change is occurring in response to change activities.

Its usefulness comes from being more explicit in saying that people are accepting the change by showing they are committing, enrolling and complying. It is less abstract and more explicit than the previous model.

Further, it gives you a clue to what you have to do to achieve the 'unfreezing'. You have to create a commitment and see that commitment being made. Later you will ask for and give people an opportunity to enrol and comply. This suggests that you need feedback mechanisms to monitor the responses you expect. Of course people may 'unfreeze' in a variety of ways, not just by showing commitment.

Questions

Are some parts of the organization more likely to make commitments, enrol and comply?

How would you tell people are committing, enrolling and complying?

Thinkers on organizational change[3] suggests that organizations are not static, so you can't, or don't even need to, 'unfreeze' them. Rather, you have to think about them as dynamic systems.

The Satir model of change

The 'Satir change model'[4] provides a more sophisticated description of the change processes. This came from Virginia Satir who was a family therapist. Her work was on change within families and the relationships between the members of the group. Her change model is often applied to organizational change.

The model (see Figure 4.1) suggests five stages of change:

1.   late status quo

2.   resistance

3.   chaos

4.   integration

5.   new status quo

2   Senge, P. (1990), *The Fifth Discipline* (London: Random House Business Books).
3   Shaw, P. (1997), 'Intervening in the shadow systems of organizations: consulting from a complexity perspective', *Journal of Organizational Change Management* 10(3).
4   Satir, V., Banmen, B. Gerber, J. and Gomori, M. (1991), *The Satir Model: Family Therapy and Beyond* (Pao Alto, CA: Science and Behaviour Books, Inc.).

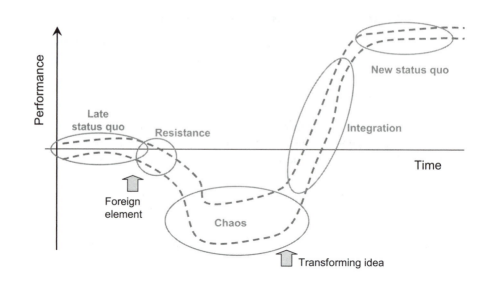

Figure 4.1   The Satir Model of Change

As can be seen in the diagram, this also describes how performance changes as the change occurs. At stage one, there is the late status quo of current performance, before some foreign element of change is brought into the situation. This might be an awareness that change is needed, competitor activity, a new chief executive or the launch of a new strategy.

Introducing this foreign element instigates a reaction of resistance, accompanied by a drop in performance. Eventually this leads to chaos where performance reaches an extremely low level. Some organizations may already be at this low level.

Now the 'transforming idea' is introduced. This provides the opportunity for change and causes performance to rise. Performance then rises to a new (hopefully higher) level, once the new idea has been integrated and the new status quo has been achieved.

The foreign element is analogous to something causing ice to melt or setting fire to a platform. It also assumes that there will be resistance and chaos, as opposed to someone saying, 'Wow, that is a great idea – let's do it!'

This model helps you think what might help people in each stage of change. At each stage, you can ask, 'What would be useful to the person during this stage?' and 'What would be useful to move them to the next stage?'

Questions

What foreign element are you introducing?

What resistance are you seeing or expecting?

What transforming idea are you bringing to the situation?

INFLUENCERS OF CHANGE

When you consider how you influence change, and how you have influenced it in the past, you may notice that a combination of effects has brought about the results. A useful way to think about how change is driven is through the three contrasting styles of change.[5] These are:

1.   normative–re-educative (social pressures)

2.   rational–empirical (logic)

3.   power–coercive (influence)

The 'normative–re-educative' approach assumes that people are social beings and will be influenced by, and adhere to, cultural and social norms. It assumes that by influencing and changing the norms and social pressures within a group, you will change their self-interests and group interests. Through these mechanisms you can re-educate and encourage people and encourage them to change their behaviour. So, if you want people to behave differently, then your attention should be on redefining and reinterpreting existing norms, behaviours and values so commitment to new ones are developed.

The 'rational–empirical' approach is based on logic and persuasion. It assumes that people are rational beings: if people can be convinced of the benefits of the change, and can see that they are real benefits, then they will be persuaded to change. The belief is that, once the benefits are revealed to them through the communication of information, the logic will be revealed, they will want to change, and change will occur.

The 'power–coercive' approach assumes people are basically compliant. They can be made to do things, or will generally do what they are told. Change is based on the exercise of authority and the imposition of sanctions. The power can be in various forms, for instance political, financial and/or emotional. You can probably think of plenty of examples where power and coercion are used to create change or even prevent it. It raises the question, 'What happens when this power or sanction is removed?'

These mechanisms of change do not occur in isolation. Think of any change situation and there will be a combination of these mechanisms operating, together, at different times, in different ways.

---

5   Bennis, W.G., Benne, K.D. and Chin, R. (eds) (1969), *The Planning of Change*, 2nd edition (New York: Holt, Rinehart and Winston).

Questions

What mechanisms of change that have been used in the past in your organization: social pressures, logic or power?

What is your change communication primarily based upon?

MIND-SETS AND MOTIVATIONS

These various models of the stages of change that people go through assume each individual is in the same frame of mind. The reality is that, whilst they may have some thinking in common, it is unlikely they are all thinking exactly the same way. So consider the motivations that people have and the mind-sets they may be in.

Bear in mind that the frame of mind people are in are often 'contextual'. Some people may have a preference for one or another way of thinking, but it will depend upon the context they are in. How they behave at work, or in a particular role, may not be how they behave at home or in other social situations. You should not assume that all people think the same way, or that an individual is always like this. People will change.

As we shall also see, mind-sets can apply to whole organizations, as well as individuals.

Internally and externally referenced

Most people use a reference point to judge how they are doing. However, they may use different types of reference points.

Some people are internally referenced. That is, they are about having a good feeling about something, *for them*. It is not something that someone else gives them, it is how *they* feel about what they did or achieved. Other people's views are either irrelevant or even without worth. Someone who feels this way may say, 'I am sure this is right,' or 'Whilst you might believe that, I believe something else' or 'Well, my gut instinct is this.' They judge themselves by their own standards.

In contrast, other people prefer an external reference point. They value the views and support of others and actively seek their opinions. You will notice that someone who frequently asks for approval will say, 'Did I do all right?', 'Was that ok?', 'Was that the right thing to do?', 'What do you think?' These people look to others as reference points. It may be about receiving recognition or praise or reward from others; equally, it may just be reassurance or confidence.

Questions

Is your preference to look for external or internal validation? Do you decide for yourself, or look for the reassurance of others?

Think of a time when you looked to, or used, the other type of reference. Why was that? How did you feel about it? (If you tend to be internally referenced, have you also sought external references?)

Of course, these preferences don't only apply to individuals. Whole organizations may demonstrate this way of thinking. Some organizations are obsessed with benchmarks and comparisons with their peers. They see their performance only relative to others. Examples often occur when there are many similar players in an industry, or where a department can find comparable functions in other organizations. This can often lead to 'me-too' strategies, where the strategy of one organization is copied from another. Some organizations see themselves as unique, trust their own judgement and are willing to be innovative. They may steal ideas from outside their industry and trust their own skills and knowledge. Still others will use a combination of internal and external points of reference, depending upon their needs at the time.

Questions

What is your reference point preference as an organization?

When you look outside for a reference, who are the points of reference?

Tangible and intangible rewards

Similarly, people and organizations have preferences for different kinds of rewards. Some rewards are tangible, such as money, promotion or a prize. Other rewards are intangible, such as how you feel about things.

Individuals may have preferences for both or either. You may feel it is important to protect people's jobs or to make sure their work is fun and enjoyable. You may also believe it is better for you and the organization financially as well, but the sense that you are doing the right thing may be the over-riding motivator.

Some people will need a minimum of extrinsic, financial reward, before they will seek out more intrinsic rewards. Others will search for a role that provides both at the same time, in some sort of balance. In caring professions particularly (nursing, palliative care and so on), individuals may choose to work for less pay because of the intrinsic satisfaction they get from the job.

The same patterns are reflected within organizations. Some organizations put considerable emphasis on, 'What is it like to work here' and 'What worth are we creating for society.' Others have a more commercial attitude to rewards.

Questions

In what circumstances do you personally prefer tangible rewards, and in what circumstances do you prefer the intangible? What does it say about you?

How does your organization motivate people?

Do you plan to appeal to people with extrinsic or intrinsic rewards?

Minimum standards

Within the many models of motivation there is often a common theme of 'hygiene' and motivation. The concept of 'hygiene factors'[6] suggests that some things, such as quality of a work environment, need to be above a certain hygiene or satisfaction level, or they will generate dissatisfaction. However, once this basic level is achieved, they no longer increase the motivation of the employee.[7] Below certain standards, they operate as a disincentive or dissatisfier. Above a certain standard they fail to operate as an additional motivator or satisfier anymore. Thus, as an office becomes more unpleasant, poorly decorated and noisy, it will demotivate. Fixing these things may improve satisfaction to a certain level; spending more beyond that will not make any difference.

The same is true with pay. As an extreme example, doubling someone's pay may act as a reward, but is unlikely to create twice as much motivation. In fact, the motivational effect is likely to be ephemeral. It doesn't take long for an individual who is rewarded this way to take their new pay scale for granted. Any reduction in pay will be highly demotivating.

> *Whilst working within an organization's change programme as an employee, an external consultant assisting in the programme asked me a question, 'If we were to cut your pay, what would your reaction be?' My reply was simple, 'I would tell you to get lost' and returned to my work.*
>
> *Like most people in employment, I have a simple view; I would be unwilling to work for an organization that decides that pay cuts are the way to make the organization successful and sustainable. This is no way to motivate the best people. I believed I could get just as well paid a role elsewhere. If the organization did not value my services, I would simply leave and go elsewhere.*

There may be a stage when people will have reached their tolerance levels for what they will put up with. At this point they may have decided to leave the organization, no matter what happens. Likewise, if things are to improve, they will need convincing it is real and will be sustained. However, that change may have no further effect above a certain improvement level.

---

6   Herzberg, F. (1968), 'One more time: how do you motivate employees?', *Harvard Business Review*, 46(1), 53–62.

7   Indeed, Taylor in the 1930s discovered that simply changing anything improved productivity as people were being paid attention to.

Questions

Are there any areas where you believe things have become intolerable?

Are there areas where people's tolerances are being tested?

Are there areas where you might be trying to raise standards too high?

Attitude to failure

It is suggested that people's attitude to failure makes a dramatic difference to their view of risk and performance. Those who are willing to take a risk and not be put off if they fail are more likely to achieve than those who are unwilling to take a risk, to risk failing and or who are worried about losing face because they have failed. The issue here is not about risk or about failing. It is about the consequences of failure. How robust is someone to the opinions of others about the failure? Are they willing to admit that they tried, failed, but got up again and tried again?

This attitude is often found amongst serial entrepreneurs and high achievers. They are not afraid to risk things and fail. Similarly, no one ever found themselves on the top of Everest or winning an Olympic Gold medal and wondered how they got there or achieved it. In other words, there is usually a goal or intention backed up by real commitment.

Questions

What is your attitude to failure?

What is your attitude to other people knowing you have failed?

What attitude to failure does the company create? Does it let people fail if they also learn, or does it punish failure?

Summary

There are many models of motivation and this section has only touched on a few. If you think people are complex, then the nature and variety of their motivations is potentially more so. Individuals will have preferred styles, but these are only preferences and these preferred styles may change with the situation they are in and what is happening at the time. Your objective may be to walk straight from one side of the jungle to the other, but when faced with a tiger, I suspect a more over-riding objective of survival and avoiding being eaten will come into your head.

Some of these motivation models are for individuals, but they can and are applied to groups and organizations. Bear these thoughts in mind as we explore the various motivations of those involved in your strategy.

'AWAY FROM' AND 'TOWARDS' THINKING

A useful model way of understanding motivation is associated with someone's orientation towards the future. Listen to an individual's pattern of conversation and try to identify whether they have an 'away from' or 'towards' view of life.

Some statements appear similar, but represent a diametric opposite. 'I want to secure people's jobs and livelihoods' has quite a different emphasis from, 'I want to avoid people being made redundant.' For some people, the incentive is avoidance or prevention of problems. For others, the incentive is achievement. These are two different ways of thinking: 'away from' and 'towards'.

'Away from' thinking

Have you ever spoken to someone who really hates their job? They will tell you all the things they *don't* want, but ask them about what they *do* want and they are often stumped. They can be very frustrating to talk to. No matter how positive you are, they seem only to talk about what they do not want or want to be.

These people are in what is called an 'away from' state of mind. They don't know what they want, as long as it is not what they have. They just want to get *away from* where they are.

We can all agree something is wrong, but not necessarily what is right. Often 'away from' people are bemused by the range of options available to them. Any way out of this hole would be good. There are so many they can't choose, so they become really stuck!

Sometimes, an 'away from' thinker may get desperate and jump to the very first opportunity that presents itself. Assuming they get past the interview question, 'Why do you want to work here?' without saying, 'because I hate my current job,' they will take up the new post and may well be unhappy there as well.

'Towards' thinking

On the other hand, you probably can think of some people who are clear about what they want. They are always telling you want they want to achieve and how they are going about it.

These people are in a 'towards' state of mind. They are moving towards something.

On occasion, 'towards' thinkers may appear unrealistic or unspecific. At other times they will be clear and will be on the lookout for opportunities to get

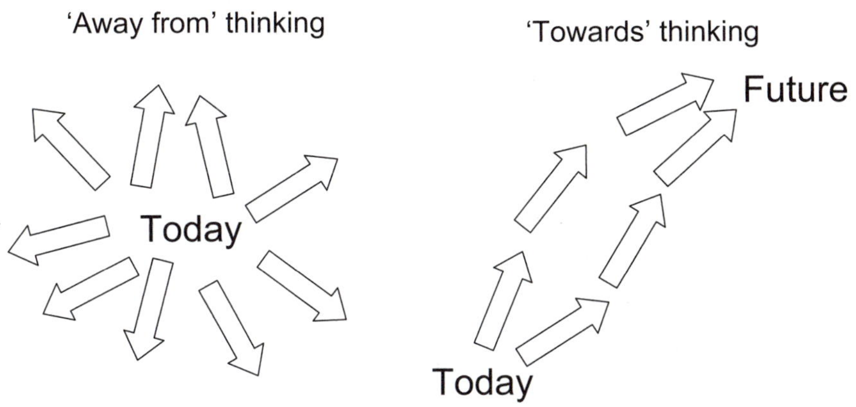

'Away from' thinking   'Towards' thinking

Today

Future

Today

Figure 4.2   'Away from' and 'Towards' thinking

them there. To the casual observer, these people may seem lucky, because opportunities appear to land in their lap. In reality, they are nothing of the sort. They are so clear about what they want, that they are able to spot and take opportunities when they appear, that others would miss. 'Towards' thinkers create their own luck.

There is a common problem with both these states of thinking; many people have problems working out what the first steps are. The 'away from' thinker does not know what to do for their first step. Anywhere will do. The 'towards' person may be talking about how good it will be when they get there, but without making the requisite practical steps towards their goal.

Questions

Listen to the language people are using. Are they 'away from' or 'towards'?

Is your preference 'towards' or 'away from'? For achieving things or preventing problems?

Think of a time when you were motivated by the opposite. Why was that? How did you feel about it?

'Away from' and 'towards' organizations

As you will have realized, this form of thinking is not exclusive to individuals. Entire organizations can develop an 'away from' mindset. I have come across business plans that spend ages telling me what the problems are and what they do not want to become (and where it was actually quite hard to find out what they did want). In contrast, some business plans are really orientated very much towards the future, but fail to acknowledge the realities of where the organization is now; all future thinking without an acceptance of the present state.

Reality is not always as clear-cut. You may have people within your organization who demonstrate both states of thinking and various degrees between the two:

- some are happy with what they have;

- some just want to change what they have, but don't know what they want;

- some want something else, and it is different from what the organization wants;

- some just want help getting out of where they are;

- some clearly know what they are trying to achieve.

Senior executives tend to be more orientated towards achievement than avoidance, which accounts for their position. They are therefore typically 'towards people'. Circumstances can lead them at times to prevent and avoid situations. They may be trying to avoid the loss of a key customer, or avoid running into cash or compliance problems.

Questions

What is the mindset of your managers?

What don't they want? What do they want to get away from?

What do they want? What do they want to move towards?

Venting

Managing this mindset is about awareness. Imagine a group of people who are very 'away from' orientated. They are fed up with what they are doing, but do not have a clear idea what to do. If you walk in and say to this group, 'Right! We are heading in this direction,' you will probably encounter resistance, for two reasons. You have not acknowledged where they are in their thinking at the moment. This is not about sharing or encouraging their despair. It is hardly helpful to say, 'You are right – we are in a mess – let's just pack in and go down the pub.'

It is about acknowledging the problems, and understanding the underlying causes that need to be put right, then moving the conversation towards more desirable situations. By acknowledging their grievances and exploring how things might be better, you are likely to take them with you. That is why it is often useful to vent.

Often, grievances are embedded in the 'away from' state of mind. When this is the case, it is necessary to listen to and acknowledge that these exist (without necessarily solving them) before you can move forward. I call this 'venting'. You give people the chance to vent their frustrations.

I was asked to take over a large project at 24 hours' notice. It had gone badly off the rails and the previous project manager had collapsed with stress. The client was furious (despite a track record of three previous failures on this project prior to our involvement).

I faced three angry clients and spent nearly 90 minutes getting beaten up with every single grievance they had coming out on the table. So much was about what was wrong. There was hardly anything about what was right, or needed to be done. When they stopped, I simply asked if there was anything else, and they would find another thing.

When I was sure they had no more, I asked for a pause.

So, at this point, I said that there were clearly mistakes in the past, but we had to work together now.

After a suitable silence, I asked them if they wanted to deliver this project (given all our jobs were resting on it).

Fortunately, I got 'yes'. Then I offered a plan that we could execute together. With their cooperation (and only with their cooperation) we could get the project on track within around 6 to 8 weeks and, from there, we would be able to estimate the actual costs and the timescale for implementation.

Fortunately, they agreed and we moved forward. Ten months later the project was being delivered on time.

Actually, I had the plan in my pocket. (I had had 24 hours notice), but there was no way I could have brought it out at the start of the meeting. It would have been shot down, ripped to shreds and blown out of the room immediately. By being patient and acknowledging their grievances, I was able to pace where they were. (Actually the project was a mess.) Having vented, and acknowledged it, we were in a position to move forward. If I had not got it all out and cleared the air, these things would have continuously come back to bite me later.

During the 2-hour meeting, they had moved from a serious 'away from' frame of mind: 'This is what is wrong with the project', to a 'towards' mindset: 'OK, we are in this together. Let's make some changes and set off on the journey.' It wasn't easy, but it was necessary and it worked.

In the end, that project went on to be very successful. What I had not realized is that their jobs were also under threat, so a solution had to be found somewhere.

Questions

What needs venting? With whom? Over what?

How can you do it constructively?

INSTIGATING CHANGE

All the previous models start with something instigating the change. This section looks at the various ways you can present the story of your current situation in a way that convinces people that change is necessary. It includes:

- creating a 'burning platform' ('when the bus leaves');
- acknowledging progress;
- explaining what will be different this time;
- demonstrating your commitment;
- what to do when the past is unacceptable;
- non-compliance, and the discipline of communication;
- taking tough decisions.

'The burning platform' and 'the leaving bus'

When starting to communicate your strategy it is important to explain where the organization is currently situated, what pressures are on it and what will happen if you continue as you are today. These explain why a new strategy is necessary.

You should also pull together facts that explain where you are today, to address the logical, rational minds. For example, how have price pressures have built up? How has the market has changed? What are customers now buying? What is the profile of your customers? Have there been any changes in the price of raw materials? And so on. The key points from a SWOT[8] analysis can be used to highlight particular aspects of the situation, picking those that support the case for your chosen strategic direction.

Your cultural survey can often be a powerful tool. Cultural surveys provide an objective assessment of how people are thinking and their frame of mind. Most reputable providers also have external benchmark information to provide you with a comparison group. They also address the emotional and peer needs of the group.

Laying out these facts builds the understanding and desire to move away from what currently exists. You are helping people realize that staying where you are is not acceptable. You are creating a metaphorical 'burning platform' from which people must jump. This is designed to act as a wake-up call for people who are happy or complacent with, or unaware of, what is happening today; to replace the, 'We are happy with where we are,' with the, 'We must move on ...' frame of mind.

---

8   SWOT analysis: strengths, weaknesses, opportunities and threats.

At a time when many organizations were downsizing, re-engineering and shedding staff, a financial services company seemed to have been passed by. Whereas many organizations at the time had a clear sense that the world was about to catch them up and they needed to change, this organization seemed to live in a secluded backwater. There was 'no fear in their eyes'.

Within 12 months a new managing director arrived and started the shake-up. It was clear from the start that changes were needed and his role was to bring them about. They employed consultants to assess the extent of the problems and the lethargy, and to bring this to the awareness of both staff and many of the managers.

At the same time, work was done on the new direction, at least in outline.

In a series of presentations, the cost comparison and mismatch in staff productivity between this company and its competitors was exposed. These created a sense of realization that things needed to be changed, whilst at the same time, the new strategy was being outlined to people. The effect was to create some immediate 'quick-win' activities to reduce costs and increase productivity, whilst the main strategy was being developed.

The turn-around in attitude, accompanied by replacing some key players in the management team, had the effect of kick-starting the organization and preparing it for the radical new strategy.

Once you have created the platform, a new 'towards' can be established: one that expresses a new strategy.

If you choose to 'set fire' to the burning platform, beware that some people will not jump and others will possibly jump either too soon, or to different places. Not everyone will choose to jump to your new platform. Nor may you want them to. It is a question of timing: when is the appropriate time to light and fan the flames of the platform?

A similar metaphor to the 'burning platform' is 'the bus is leaving'.[9] This suggests that the organization is moving forward with the new strategy and you have a choice about whether to be on it, commit or be left behind. The burning platform suggests a necessary compulsion to jump, or be burnt, both of which could be unpleasant. The leaving bus suggests choice. You can choose to stay at the bus stop, but we are starting a journey and there won't be a second chance.

Of course the bus may pause after a while to get rid of some passengers it is carrying who don't wish to make the journey. It may also pick up new passengers on the way as the journey unfolds. However, unlike most buses, it has no intention of returning to the bus terminus from which it left.

---

9   Collins, J.C. and Porras, J.I. (1989), *Built to Last* (London: Random House Business Books). This has a useful section that uses the bus is leaving metaphor for organizations developing the right management team.

The 'burning platform' or 'leaving bus' is a part of your story. Whichever you choose to use, you are communicating to your managers and staff the imperative for change.

Questions

'The burning platform':

- *Do you need to create a burning platform to awaken complacency, or will people move with you without it?*

- *If you do need one, what evidence do you have? What will set the platform alight?*

- *How quickly do you want to fan the flames? When will the new platform be available? How will you provide the new platform for people to move to, and the bridge for people to move across?*

'The leaving bus':

- *When is your bus leaving?*

- *How many seats are there?*

- *How will you demonstrate this?*

Acknowledging progress

By reading this book you have already started on your journey to communicate your strategy more effectively. You will already have had insights and ideas that will help you improve how you will do it, and you will have realized what assets and resources are at your disposal.

As the last paragraph demonstrates, there is value in acknowledging the progress that has already been made.

> *Whilst reviewing the strategy with the board of a large corporate we were talking about the next steps that people had identified. There was some discomfort in the room. Then one of the directors interrupted, 'You know we have made massive progress over the last 4 years don't you?'*
>
> *This surprised us. It was not an issue that had come up in the interviews and discussions. It was only later we realized that, even in the boardroom, there was a degree of resentment that the substantial improvements to the supply chain and other parts of the organization had not been acknowledged.*

This was an example of wanting to be acknowledged. The management team had moved their organization (possibly kicking and screaming) from being a 'three out of ten' organization to a 'seven out of ten' organization. Now it seemed we were changing the goalposts and saying that they only scored 'seven out of twelve', as they still had further to go.

In some organizations there is often a degree of what appears to be change fatigue. Having just got over the last major change initiative, employees are hurled directly into the new one. It is often said that the rate of change is getting faster. I'm not sure if this is true, or if the rate at which changes are made is getting faster. Either way, most people in organizations have been subject to a series of change initiatives. Therefore, acknowledging the progress they have made so far is important. It is a way of saying, 'Well done! We have achieved a lot, and here is the next step we would like your help with.'

Some organizations suffer from repeated change that has not been embedded. When you ask them about a new idea, they will tell you about a change (or management fad) that was implemented several years ago, to much razzamatazz, only to die out some months or years later. In this case, it is helpful to say, 'You know, 3 years ago we were here and we have made terrific progress. Now things have moved on again and we are at the next stage in this journey.' Of course, if you are going to say this you had better ensure the journey has a direction and is not going around in circles.

The outside world will also have changed. Three years ago the benchmark price for a mobile phone might have been £130 and it is now £70, and has twice as many features. Perhaps the supply chain standard was 10 days' inventory and is now down to four. The target you were heading towards has moved away from you. In these cases it is important to acknowledge the progress, as well as set the new standards to be met.

This process of acknowledgement is particularly significant when a new management team is involved. As a new manager in an organization you will not have lived through the previous changes. You may be aware of the changes and may have lived through changes you and others have instigated in different organizations, but you did not live through these particular changes. In this case, it is helpful to acknowledge where people have come from and appreciate what people have gone through; to acknowledge it and to acknowledge where people have come from, just as it is important to highlight the gap between where they are today and where they need to be.

Questions

Where was this organization 3 years and 1 year ago?

What changes has it achieved in the recent past?

Explaining what will be different, this time

As we have already discussed, some organizations have a track record of failed change. This can build up an attitude of 'not another change programme'.

While working with an organization to help them improve their strategic planning, an initial review quickly brought up some pockets of resistance.

It quickly became apparent that there were many different practices around the organization. Moreover, different parts of the organization operated quite autonomously. When asked about past experience, it transpired that there had been least five different initiatives over the past 12 years, all of which were attempting to introduce a common strategic planning process across the organization.

The message was clear: we had to work out what the underlying issue was. What was the common thread that had stopped previous changes? We also had to ensure that we made it clear that this time was different; not by adopting a different approach, but by adopting one that would address the underlying problems, problems that were deep seated – otherwise we would not be credible.

Questions

Look for patterns of failed change. What has stopped change happening in the past?

How can we be different this time and show we are being different?

How will you convince others that this time will be different?

In the case above, there was no incentive for individual mangers to follow the common line. There was little central power being wielded and individual directors were allowed to follow their own paths. Until people were held accountable to the centre and responsible for consistent planning so the pieces could be integrated, people were going to do their own thing. Sometimes you may even have to sack someone to demonstrate you are serious.

Demonstrating your commitment

Of course you don't have to start by sacking people. There are other ways to show you are serious. The duration, integrity, commitment, effort (DICE)[10] model for assessing change provides a useful way to think about this. The originators report that this model provides a very reliable predictor of the success of a change project or programme. It also makes explicit what needs to be improved.

The *duration* between reviews makes a significant difference. If you do not follow up with progress reviews on a regular basis, or you leave it a long time between reviews, people will not take you seriously. Having major progress reviews of a strategy project more than 2 months apart starts to weaken the credibility of the reporting process: monthly would keep everyone on top of the project. The reporting process should also have:

- clear timescales

- clear milestones

- expected results

---

10   Sirkin, H.L., Keenan, P. and Jackson, A. (2005), 'The Hard Side of Change Management', *Harvard Business Review* (October), Harvard Business Online.

Scheduling milestones, gaining commitment to them and tracking progress are the simplest ways to ensure a project's progress. You may encounter some resistance, but there are ways to overcome it.

> *'I made it clear,' explained the managing director, 'I needed costs cutting and I wanted 10 per cent cuts to be brought to the next meeting. If they did not find them, I would find them for them: it was their choice. They had 2 months to come up with them.'*
>
> *It was as much about ensuring they understood I was serious, as it was about their demonstrating that they were willing to change.*

Such progress reviews should be formal meetings, not informal 'how are we progressing' updates. You can do these as well, but still hold the formal ones. People should also be clear about what they are expected to deliver. Inconsistent follow-ups will undermine progress. In contrast, being able to demonstrate tangible progress will support the change.

The *integrity* of the team dedicated to the project will make a difference. How motivated are they? Do they have the right skills? Do they have sufficient time for the change programme? Do they believe it is achievable? If employees look at the project team and think they are not a credible group, their work will be sunk at the start.

The extent to which *commitment* is explicit from both managers and employees also makes a difference. Are senior managers actively communicating the importance of the changes and the reasons behind the change? Are they demonstrating commitment by putting resources behind it themselves and communicating a coherent message? Is there employee commitment? Do the people affected by the change understand the reasons behind it? Are they convinced about the changes? Are they supporting it or undermining it?

Finally, the amount of *effort* that people are able to put into a change programme alongside their existing work is also a factor. If people are expected to continue to put 110 per cent into their existing jobs *and* spend 3 to 4 days a week on the new change programme, something has to give way. It will be one of the existing work, the project or the person.

WHEN THE PAST IS UNACCEPTABLE

Sometimes senior management has to demonstrate explicitly that past performance and behaviour is unacceptable. If past changes have systematically been a failure, do not prevaricate. Confront the issues and explain that *how changes are made* needs to change.

An organization had a £150 million budget yet did not know what projects were being run in the various parts of the organization. Directors operated fiefdoms and kept their changes to themselves. No one had the overall costs of these projects.

The directors in each fiefdom did not appear to know the situation in their area. We set out to identify these projects and get a clear list. However, we were confronted with all sorts of excuses, including being asked to define 'a project' (these were experienced directors) and asking for time whilst people created lists.

It took over 6 weeks and a lot of chasing to get a list of 140 projects around the organization (and even then we knew it was not complete). Still, many had no business cases, no costs, no statements of benefits, no project managers and unclear timescales and responsibilities, let alone funding. Much was being done alongside business as usual.

By simply putting all the projects on a single sheet of paper in front of all the directors, we were able to expose the true size of the problem and bring out any missing or hidden projects.

The exercise was part of a larger cultural change project aimed at improving performance and accountability. Here we were discovering how big the existing change programme was and the size of the accountability problem.

By getting to this stage, we were able to give the directors an overall picture of what was going on in their own areas, as well as between areas. This became the starting point for establishing a programme management team to oversee programmes in the future.

But the real issue was cultural. A new deputy chief executive arrived and instigated a stronger routine. At the first meeting, he asked for progress on a major project. He received nothing in the meeting. The same thing happened in the second meeting. So he made it clear: 'Failure to provide the information would be considered a disciplinary issue.'

Guess what? The project information appeared. Afterwards, the central programme management team had clearer information and greater cooperation. Individual directors were made responsible for programmes of work across departments and were expected to demonstrate progress.

People could see progress. There was transparency, responsibility and accountability.

In this organization people were allowed to get away with it. The new deputy chief executive made it clear that this was no longer acceptable. Things were going to change, or else!

Questions

Where do you need to confront changes?

Where is the past no longer acceptable?

How can you raise and confront these issues?

If you fail to address these issues, they will continue to undermine your success, credibility and results, just as they have undermined people, and the strategy, previously.

The discipline of communication

Sometimes you have to carry a big stick to get attention and to get the message across.

> *Many years ago (and I emphasize many years ago), I met a really effective project manager. He was about six foot two inches tall and broadly built. He was a lovely guy with a really pleasant manner. He was also very disciplined about tasks being completed and actions being followed up. He carried a pad and constantly wrote down agreed actions, so he could follow them up.*
>
> *He also carried a big stick, literally. From somewhere around the office he had found a piece of wood, roughly two inches by two inches and about three foot long. He carried it on his shoulder and would walk into meetings, place it on the table with a smile and simply say, 'So what progress have we made today?' He literally carried a big stick. Whilst he never used it, and didn't need to carry it for long, the implication was for all to see. He was so effective that the company later employed him as their IT director.*

Similarly, a long time ago I met a finance director who kept a flick knife on his desk as a paperweight. I was told he would play with it in meetings. He was sending out a clear message. Of course, literally carrying a big stick or playing with a flick knife in meetings is unacceptable today. However, it is allowed metaphorically.

When you are communicating and implementing a change programme you will come up against resistance. Sometimes it is due to inertia or because the programme is not being taken seriously. Sometimes there will be malicious compliance: appearing to go along with the change programme, leaving meetings agreeing to actions and then undermining them.

> *The managing director described how the old management he had inherited would either brief against the programme outside the boardroom, or simply find ways to not comply, fail to deliver or fail to brief their people. Other times they would make excuses for why change was not being carried through.*
>
> *When presenting to a group of middle managers, he made an off the cuff remark that the cultural survey seemed to suggest that the cultural problem was with the senior management and board, 'If we simply sacked them all that would seem to make a big difference.' This got resounding cheers.*

Within 6 months half of the original management team and senior managers had left and within 2 years only two remained. Meanwhile a dramatic cultural change had been achieved.

Sometimes there will be simple non-compliance.

In the NHS, a significant contributor to preventing cross-infection amongst patients is thought to be the cleanliness of wards and hospital staff. Washing hands has been identified as a major element of this. A director in the NHS described how they had signs up everywhere in his hospital to remind people to wash their hands. They even had it as a screen saver on everyone's PCs.

Of course, as he pointed out, this is a classic piece of wrong thinking. People should not need reminding that they need to wash their hands thoroughly. After all, these are trained medical staff. They should know they have to maintain cleanliness and hygiene. Moreover, they should want to. Yet we still have problems. 'I suspect,' he mused, 'that if we disciplined a couple of people for failing to wash their hands, we would quickly get the message across, change attitudes and lower infection rates. At the same time we would not need all these silly signs.'

If you take this route, be careful to ensure you have complied with contract and employment law. If it results in a constructive dismissal case, it can be very expensive. On the other hand, there are ways to remove employees who are underperforming, and it may be wise to take appropriate employment law advice early.

Questions

What sort of resistance are you up against?

What are you going to do about it?

Are you going to be taken seriously?

Are you going to need 'a big stick', or something more subtle?

You have to demonstrate you are serious. How can you do that?

Tough decisions

Directors and managers sometimes simply have to tell people to get on with it. At times you may have to make a tough decision: to make people redundant, close down plants, move services offshore, move manufacturing facilities or shed unprofitable customers.

Of course, you will need to plan these changes carefully. You will need to comply with statutory requirements and contractual conditions. There are statutory redundancy periods and notice periods to comply with. There may also be consultation arrangements with unions and worker representative groups. In some countries this will include a workers' executive, in others the union, or a workers' representative panel or group.

Some employers will stick with statutory minimum terms for redundancies. Others may decide to offer preferential terms to all or particular groups of staff.

You may decide to put in place counselling, job assistance or support for any people made redundant. You may even be eligible for funding from government depending upon where you are located. Some organizations help their ex-employees start new businesses, so they become or move to suppliers, customers and competitors. Remember, these people will continue to talk with people in your industry and with customers and suppliers. They will continue to be ambassadors for your company, whether you employ them or not. How you treat them will be reflected back on you as an organization.

Questions

What statutory or compulsory arrangements do you have to make?

What contractual obligations do you have?

What are you doing to help and how are you communicating this help to these people?

How are you ensuring that those people who leave remain ambassadors for your company?

While attention is paid to those being made redundant, you also need to talk with the 'survivors'. They might be relieved they are still in a job. They might wish they were offered a redundancy cheque. They might simply fear that they will be included in the next round of redundancies.

On occasion, when people leave an organization quickly, with no notice, sometimes those who remain are asked not to contact those who have left. I do find this strange, but it is not unusual. I have personally witnessed it twice. In one case people were explicitly asked not to contact those that had left. It is almost as if the management were saying, 'Those people are bad and you are the survivors. Do not mix with them.' In reality, these people were probably your friends and will remain so long after they have left.

You will also notice that some of the 'survivors', perhaps when the cuts seem somewhat arbitrary, are embarrassed that they still have a job. You get a double whammy: rejected by your company and rejected by your ex-workers.

You will probably have selected key people you are keen to retain. If you handle the redundancies poorly, you may disenfranchise them as well. Handle this badly, and they will simply leave when they are ready, on their terms.

The message is simple: pay attention to what messages and signals you send out, both to those who are leaving and to those who remain.

Questions

How will you deal with the survivors?

How will you manage the message to them?

How will you make sure they do not leave at the soonest opportunity as well?

A CHANGE MODEL

We have covered a variety of models of change and some of the thinking and processes associated with them. No single approach is appropriate in all circumstances. The balance you need to adopt between the options and approaches will be down to your judgement.

Whatever approach to change you adopt, you are likely to include the following elements:

1. create realization, awareness, understanding and urgency;

2. ask for commitment and show you expect it;

3. describe a future, new way of working, so that people can relate to it;

4. foster and support commitment to the new values;

5. explicitly eliminate resistance and malicious compliance;

6. build a social pressure within the organization;

7. institutionalize the new ways of working.

This list is not designed as a prescriptive or sequential model. It is more a checklist of the elements of change you are likely to need. You will notice how it incorporates all the elements of the different models we have discussed. At any time in the process you may be using a combination of these together.

This list provides a checklist from which you can choose the tools you need, from this chapter and your own experience, to make sure the change is communicated, understood and implemented.

CONCLUSION

The emphasis in this chapter has been that 'strategy is about change'. We have explored the explicit mechanisms of change that you might employ. One of the reasons strategy sometimes fails is that the people who are trying to create a change are unclear about what mechanisms of change they are using.

Some models have described the stages of change as if they were simply describing the change of a caterpillar into a pupa and then into a butterfly. Others help you understand peoples' state of readiness for change and what might be stopping them from changing. Yet other models provide tools that help you influence, control, manage, monitor and acknowledge the change process.

Most of these approaches rely on persuasion, logic, social pressure or appealing to someone's better judgement. There will, however, be times when the past is unacceptable, when people persist in unhelpful or unconstructive behaviours, or when you simply need to make it clear that 'the bus is leaving' and they need to choose whether to get on or be left behind. You will also need to carry a metaphorical 'big stick' and be prepared to use it: merely carrying one will communicate a message.

Sometimes a symbolic action will communicate a much stronger message than you will ever be able to communicate verbally. You have to be ready for the consequences and be sure of your legal ground.

5 'What's in it for...?'

Whilst you may be extolling the benefits of this strategy, others may be thinking, 'That's all jolly well, but what's in it for me?'

Some of them are also thinking, 'What's in it for you?' What is in it for you, the reader? Presumably you are reading this because you wish to communicate a strategy. How you think about things will influence how you communicate them.

In the last chapter we explored general motivations. In this chapter we will explore the specific motivations and thinking of various players. They include:

- staff

- union and worker representation

- customers

- suppliers

- investors

- regulatory bodies

- political and pressure groups

To be successful at understanding, 'What's in it for them', you have to be able to think through other peoples' motivations, from *their* perspective. Put yourself in the other person's shoes and think as if you are that other person. This is not thinking what they *might* want. It is thinking what they are thinking and what they want, as if you were them. The better you are able to do this, the greater the understanding you will have of their situation. This chapter starts by explaining some of the techniques you can use to do this.

THINKING 'AS IF YOU WERE THEM'

Throughout this chapter there are two key techniques to employ, techniques that increase your ability to empathize with others dramatically. The first involves thinking 'as if you were' the other person. The second involves developing archetypes of the people with whom you will be communicating. Both techniques will help you understand the players and so communicate more effectively.

'As if you were them'

When I work with a client I often ask, 'What do your customers want?' The usual reply starts with, 'They want … '. The respondee is answering from their own perspective, rather than from the perspective of the customer. Thinking and talking about something from your perspective is called being in 'first position'.

Answering from the other person's perspective, as if you were them, is called being in 'second position'. The key to this approach is to say and write things down as if you were them. Start sentences with, 'I want … ' or 'I would like.' In each case, the 'I' refers to the person you are seeking to understand.

Understanding this is vital to getting inside the thinking of *that* person, rather than being in your own head. Have in mind an individual. You are taking on *their* beliefs, thinking, lifestyle and needs; therefore, you should act and think as if you were that person. See the world from that individual's perspective.

Stereotypes and archetypes

When clients first try to answer these questions, they try to answer the question for the whole of a group of representative people. The problem is that groups often have diverse needs, so you need to choose specific individuals to think about.

Be specific about which individual you are dealing with. Write down their characteristics and details. This helps tremendously when a group of you are doing this together. If you think you are being the same person but are thinking as if you are different people, you are will get confusion. For example, when you are dealing with an organization, choose whom specifically you are talking about. The perspective of the managing director is likely to be different from the purchasing manager, who may again be different from the actual user. These people will have different perspectives. Treat them as individuals and think about each of them separately.

Where you have a group of people, such as project managers, to consider, it is sometimes more effective to take an individual from each group, develop the thinking for that individual, and then explore other individuals from the group, looking for similarities and differences. This way you build up a richer picture. You also avoid arguments where you are discussing different facets of different customers in the same group.

Some critics say that this approach is stereotyping. Rather, think of this as developing an archetype or archetypes: social and demographic analysis has been doing this for years. Stereotypes and archetypes are quite different. A stereotype suggests everyone is the same and typecasts them. In contrast, an archetype contains the essential elements of that group. Members may, of course, differ from this archetype. Identifying these differences, and why they occur, provides valuable insights.

The more you can make these archetypes real, for yourself and each other, without stereotyping, the better the quality of understanding you will develop.

Questions

What groups have you identified? Who might be archetypes of those groups? For each of the archetypes:

Think as if you were them. What would they want?

What experience do you have of the groups with whom you want to communicate?

Do you have enough information to think 'as if you were them'? If not, who should you involve who could provide these insights?

'WHAT'S IN IT FOR ME?' (WIIFM)

This may seem a strange place to start, but it is valuable to recognize your own motives in this communication. By asking yourself, 'What's in it for me?', you will start to get inside your own head and make your own assumptions explicit. Your answers may be different depending upon the role you play.

If you are a senior manager or director responsible for designing the strategy, then the strategy may be something personal to you. Not only have you toiled emotionally and intellectually on the subjects, you have probably had long and detailed discussions with your colleagues, resolving details, reconciling contrary information or positions and coming to a consensus with which you are happy.

You may well have strong financial incentives tied to the results. Many directors' remuneration is closely linked to share price performance through bonus payments or through share option and purchase schemes. Others may be paid by results. Perhaps you believe that your future reputation or earnings potential is intimately tied to the success of this strategy. In the view of the city investors, your name is intimately linked with the recovery, change or turnaround.

Table 5.1 shows some things that may drive a director's motivation, either as a desire to achieve or a desire to avoid.

If you are a senior or middle manager, you may have some motivators that are similar and some that come from a different perspective. Your particular list may vary depending upon the ownership and incentive schemes in place. Perhaps you were involved in the strategy's evolution and development. Perhaps you have arrived as part of the team brought in by the new management. You may have explicit incentives linked to the strategy. Amazingly though, research suggests that while 74 per cent of senior executives had their compensation linked to the organization's goals, fewer than one-third reported incentives linked to long-term strategic objectives and fewer than 10 per cent of middle managers and front line employees have their incentives linked in this way.[1]

If you are in a role of communications, perhaps in marketing, internal communications or the strategy team, your motivations may be different. You are more likely to be acting as a facilitator, or perhaps the messenger rather than the proponent and source of the strategy. Your role will be to help the strategy be communicated. No matter what your role, it is worth understanding, 'What's in it *for me*?' and, 'Why is getting this right important, *for me*?'

Table 5.1   What's in it for me?

Potential gains	Potential losses
• Financial rewards	• Financial loss
• Share options	• Missed share opportunities
• Personal investment return	• Loss of investment in the business
• Building kudos	
• Long-term reputation	• Saving face
• Enhancing career prospects	• Potentially losing the business
• Adding a key success to your CV	• Undermining your career prospects
• Building a reputation as a management team	• Avoiding a failure on your CV
	• Not letting down the management team you are in
• Saving people's jobs	• Seeing people made redundant
• Ensuring employment in the community	• Having an adverse effect on the community
• The reputation of the business	
• Securing control of the business	• Loss of pension
• Protection from take-overs	• Loss of ownership of the business
• Growth in shareholder returns	• Loss of control to a rival business
	• Loss of value for shareholders

1   Norton, D.P. and Kaplan, R.S. (1996), *The Balanced Scorecard: Translating Strategy into Action* (Boston, Massachusetts: Harvard Business School Press).

Questions

What is in it for you?

Why is this important to you?

What outcomes do you want to avoid?

What will you get out of this if it succeeds?

What do others think is in it for you?

WHAT'S IN IT FOR THE STAFF?

Given there will be so many different groups, constituencies and parts of your workforce, it is inappropriate to generalize about how they will be affected.

As a basic need, most of your workers will be thinking about job security. With increasing trends to outsource and overseas working, employees may feel insecure when change occurs. This will not be true for all employees. Some may regard themselves as part of a valuable profession, such as IT, rather than as employed by the company, and may believe they can easily move their services to another company. Others may feel that their jobs are threatened by change.

Even though someone's job may not be threatened, organizational change can alter their career plans. People may be expecting to make a move to a particular department, or anticipate a promotional opportunity, only to see it disappear with a change. This can happen at any level in the organization.

> *The IT director saw his chance to move into general management and devoted a lot of time helping to develop the strategy for the new direct insurance operation. Plans were so advanced, and his move to lead the new operation so assured, that his replacement was being recruited. However, a new managing director arrived to head up the overall company and almost immediately stopped work on the direct operation. The IT director was left in limbo. He had started his move away from managing his department, a replacement was on the way and his new role disappeared. Within 4 months he was working for a different company.*

One aspect of organizational change and new strategy that needs careful management is any change to the reward scheme. If you have had a set of objectives established at the beginning of the year, and a new strategy is launched mid-year, where do your objectives now sit? What has happened to the objectives on which your bonus rested? The same may be true for any bonus arrangements that are in place. In some cases it may be appropriate to pay the bonuses based upon past performance. In others it may be necessary to set or renegotiate the objectives. In extreme circumstances, the opportunity for a bonus may disappear completely if the performance of the business has been so poor as to necessitate it.

Staff who work in a particular location may be concerned about an office move. If an office is to close, the staff may be relocated to a new office or offered a severance. Having warning of closure gives people time to find a new job or make alternative travelling arrangements.

> *'It's better to have the certainty of bad news, than the uncertainty,' declared the managing director. When we closed the office, we gave people about 18-months' notice that it was going to be closed. By the time it closed, everyone was sorted. Those affected saw it as a massive plus that they'd had their redundancies and started new jobs.*

74

People who work remotely, such as regional sales or service staff and homeworkers, will have a different problem. They may be separate from the main office and perhaps visit it only once a month, if at all. Their connection with the main organization may be by phone, email or video conference. In these circumstances, changes in the organization's strategy will need to be carefully communicated to them as their rumour mill and personal network will work far more quickly than the official lines of communication.

As an example of poor communication and consultation, there was outrage when an injury claims firm decided to sack its workers by text message.

> *The UK's largest personal injury claims firm, Accident Group, has sacked 2 400 people – many by text message – after its parent company Amulet Group announced on Friday that it would go into administration. Staff with company mobile phones received a series of text messages, warning them that salaries would not be paid. Manchester-based Amulet Group said its subsidiary had to cease trading because it could not sustain its 'continual battles with the insurance industry' and after 'the sudden failure of a banking partner to support the company.'*

> *The administrators, though, blame Accident Group's 'lower than expected claims success rate' for the financial difficulties, which they say 'resulted in increased insurance premiums on new business and retrospective claims from the underwriters.'[2]*

However, this case had a happier ending, which also provides a salutary lesson for companies.

> *Twenty-one former workers with the Accident Group, who were sacked by text message by the now-defunct claims company, were awarded compensation*

---

2   BBC website, 'Bust company sacks workers by text', 30 May 2003 <http://news.bbc.co.uk/1/hi/business/2949578.stm>.

at an employment tribunal on Wednesday. It found they had been 'cynically manipulated'.

The no-win, no-fee injuries claims company collapsed in May this year (2003), with debts of more than £30 million, including unpaid wages. The first that many of its employees knew of the problems was when a text message was sent to their mobile phones indicating that their wages would not be paid.

Twenty-one employees brought a test case before an employment tribunal, claiming what is known as a 'protection award': a statutory payment by the Government amounting to £260 per week, for 90-days work, in lieu of notice. The tribunal in Ashford granted the awards after finding that the senior management knew since January (2003) that the company was unlikely to survive. Tribunal chairman Anthony Druce said, 'The staff were being cynically manipulated to keep the company running until the last moment.'

He concluded, 'There was no attempt at consultation so we, therefore, find that the claim is successful.'[3]

The moral of this story is that remote and homeworkers, especially, need proper consultation processes when major changes occur. Being sacked is an extreme form of change of working arrangements. Other less drastic changes still require consultation and appropriate communication.

Of course, not all change is bad. Remember, it is not change that people dislike; it is feeling that they have not being involved, consulted or are unable to influence change that they find most frustrating. So the message should be, 'Consult me, give me notice, treat me with respect and give me a chance to understand and influence the change.'

Many changes are an opportunity. If you have been working in a frustrating environment, and a new managing director offers to make drastic changes to improve the organization, to free up people's capabilities and make it a much better place to work, many are likely to take notice. It presents an opportunity for a better working life.

UNION AND WORKER REPRESENTATION

The ACAS advisory booklet[4] on worker consultation and representation states, 'Involvement of employee representatives can encourage understanding, trust, better decision making and improve employment relations as well as improving organizational effectiveness.' It suggests that, 'The day-to-day relations between managers and workers are greatly enhanced by effective systems of representation and consultation between

---

3   Article on the website of an international law firm, Pinsent Masons, December 2003, www. out-law.com/page-4152.

4   ACAS, advisory booklet 'Representation at work', www.acas.org.uk.

managers and worker representatives.' It also adds, 'Whether or not they are excluded from legal requirements it is good practice for firms of all sizes to have effective systems for providing information to and consulting with their employees.'

Worker representation has traditionally been dominated by trade unions, but with the decline in union membership other forms of representation are increasingly significant. The employer lobby has sometimes opposed the involvement of unions on the grounds of time constraints and a preference for informal employee relations. For example, in the public consultation exercise reviewing the Employment Relations Act 1999, the British Printing Industries Federation stated that, according to its estimates, a small company could lose up to 50 per cent of its profit margins as a result of going through the recognition procedure.[5] Whilst this seems extreme, poor employee relations have cost some organizations dearly.

In the absence of formal structures and practices, the opportunities for workers in small firms to have their interests represented and to voice their concerns may be limited. In contrast, some would argue that, in a small firm, it is far easier to get your voice heard.

Where there are formal agreements in place, there will be strict timescales for consultation prior to actions. In all cases, the worker representations and various unions provide a useful channel through to your staff, which should be used as thoroughly as any other channel.

Good relationships with unions and worker representation groups can pay enormous dividends and they should be seen as a positive and beneficial channel of communication. Having your union representatives alongside, agreeing with the strategy and supporting it, should send a very positive message to the workforce they represent.

Questions

What are the formal mechanisms of employee representation in your company?

What statutory requirements do you have?

What formal and informal arrangements do you have in place?

How effective are these at communicating with the various parts of your workforce?

Who else also needs to know?

---

5   European industrial relations observatory on-line, article, www.eiro.eurofound.ie/2004/12/feature/uk0412105f.html.

WHAT'S IN IT FOR THE CUSTOMERS?

Many organizations explain their strategy in terms of what they do, for instance, 'We make cars.' Some organizations explain their strategy in terms of what they will do for the customer, 'We make cars that are economic and reliable to drive.'

But some go further. They realize what matters is what it *means* for the customers. The questions that should be at the front of their mind are, 'What will be the customers' experience?' or 'How will they benefit?' From their position, 'What would I want?':

'I want my work colleagues to be envious of my car.'

'I want a car that costs as little as possible and one where my grandmother can get in the back.'

'I want to do the school run safely.'

Marketers used to believe that share of market drove profitability. Now they believe that it is share of the customer's mind. Share of mind is driven by experience. For example, think of search engines, online auction sites and music players that begin with 'i'. I suspect you can guess who I am thinking of in each of these cases. These examples (Google, eBay, iPod) have become synonymous with search engines, online auctions and MP3 players. They have a share of your mind and, therefore, your pocket.

Some organizations still talk of their product features when they describe their product. Others are talking about the benefits that the features provide or the experience that they provide for customers.

It is the whole experience that matters. My car experience includes purchasing, servicing, getting spares and asking for advice, but it is mainly about driving it and relying on it to get me to clients when I need it. It is good to have nice coffee at the car dealership, but I would prefer not to be there at all.

People will have had a reason to buy from you. Sometimes they are simply making a commodity purchase, but sometimes their motivation may be what you stand for in their mind as well as what value you add.

Be very careful of over-analyzing your customers and markets. It has been said[6] that markets are collections of individuals, classified together for the convenience of an organization. Ensure that you think of your customers as

---

6   Levin, Locke, Searls, Weinberger (1999), *The Cluetrain Manifesto* (Perseus Books). See www. cluetrain.com/#manifesto for the manifesto, or www.cluetrain.com/book/index.html to read the whole book online.

individuals who perhaps some share common characteristics that enable you to treat them as a group.

Questions

What change will this strategy make to your customers?

What evidence do you have for that belief?

A further consideration is the availability of channels of communication to your customers. Whilst some will have direct relationships with your organization, say business to business companies, others may not. A car manufacturer's direct customers are dealers, leasing companies and fleet purchasers. Its end users only deal with them through intermediaries, and then only rarely. So its communications tend to be through other channels such as the media, trade shows, car magazines, and even the licensing authority if a recall is necessary.

On the other hand some customers are getting close to companies through affiliation with their website. How often are you asked to register a new electronic product on the Internet and provide your email? It makes no difference to the warranty, but does mean you can get downloads and updates, and it means that the company has a direct route to its customers' inboxes.

WHAT'S IN IT FOR THE SUPPLIERS?

You will have many forms of supplier. Some suppliers may be suppliers of commodity items and therefore not of significance to the strategy. Others are important, perhaps providing large components, and therefore your decisions will have an effect on their business. Some of these may be effective partners where you may have been doing joint development or have integrated supply chains, or they may provide a specific and critical component of your offering.

You will not need to communicate your strategy to all suppliers unless you are undergoing a large supplier rationalization, or moving them all on to a new supply chain arrangement.

On the other hand, there may be some suppliers, with whom you work closely, who are particularly affected by the strategy. For these suppliers, you may choose to have a communication programme that runs alongside the main change programme.

A large company was undergoing a major change programme to improve its service to customers and increase its efficiency. It wrote to all its major suppliers to explain the reason for the change programme and the changes that were being introduced. Initially, this was a short letter outlining the change of emphasis and the core areas they were trying to improve for their customers. Following on from this, as the change programme developed, specific initiatives and negotiations that involved the various suppliers were implemented, with the cooperation of the suppliers. The end result was a far better arrangement for all parties.

Bear in mind that, from the supplier's perspective, you might not be an attractive customer. This may come as a surprise to many organizations, but there comes a point when some suppliers, forced to compete solely on price, may not welcome your business anymore. Similarly, a supplier may have moved into new markets and only be supplying you as a source of cash income that is not as 'strategic' or important to them as perhaps their other customers now are. In the same way that you will do customer segmentation, so will they.

Questions

What do your suppliers need to know?

When should you tell them?

How do they view you?

What reaction do you expect?

INVESTORS

You need to take care when dealing with the investor community. Investors, in this context, can be a variety of people.

If you are a publicly listed company, then your investment community will mainly consist of fund managers, analysts and pension funds. It may also include sophisticated day-traders based at home and individual web-based investors with relatively stable portfolios. You will also be subject to regulatory requirements on your reporting.

If you are not listed, different rules may apply. If you are looking for investment from venture capital, angel investors, or some sort of venture fund or mezzanine finance, you will need to put together specific investor information for that purpose.

If you are a family business, then your investors can be parents, brothers and sisters, or other close family. A family firm with a closed investor community may have no published investor relation information at all, apart from its statutory accounts.

If you are funded by private equity, your investors may include large venture capital or private equity funds, or individual angel investors.

Even a charity will have investor relations. Charities will be complying with statutory requirements applicable to their status. Donors are investors in a way. The charity may be looking for large investors or donors, as well as small ones, to fund specific projects and therefore want to publish specific information to attract them, show them how their funds could be used, or help the donors understand how their money has been used.

This even applies in the public sector. Public sector organizations rely on grants, taxes and funding from government, the public and other bodies. So, they too need to ensure that these 'investors' have confidence in the management and their plans as well as the delivery of the services.

It is claimed that you can improve the value of your organization by simply having better relationships with your investors. This seems surprising, but it is true. The limited liquidity of some shares precludes trade and therefore limits the realizable value. Investors like transparency and liquidity. The clearer your communications, the easier it is for them to understand them and trust them. Even if there is bad news, explaining the bad news well will engender trust and understanding. Try to avoid delivering bad news too often, though.

Investor communication should enhance an investor's or a shareholder's understanding of the company and its market. To do this, many organizations use their website as a key source of data. Therefore, ensure your company, its publications and its website are the definitive source of information on your company. This should include clear and comprehensive financial information. This is especially important for a listed company. You should also ensure equality of access to information to ensure you cannot be accused of favouring particular investor groups.

From the investors' perspective, they are likely to have several objectives:

- trust in the information;
- trust in the persistent quality of the information and forecasts;
- clarity and transparency of the information;
- ready comparison with peers and other players in the market;
- access to the data in a standard form, so that they can do easy comparisons;
- reliability of future forecasts;
- developing an understanding of the management and their thinking and style;
- regulatory compliance.

You need to ensure you comply with the regulatory requirements of the regime in which you operate, and how you comply with IFRS[7] or Sarbanes-Oxley.[8]

Beware – there are statutory requirements for disclosure in listed companies. Therefore external disclosures that could be treated as market information are required to follow specific rules. Make sure that these are followed. Get advice from your advisor on investor relations.

On the subject of investor relations, how many times have you heard of a large share price movement happening when a company's results have underperformed against what the market and investors expected? The key is to keep them informed. Managing their expectations is too much of a cliché, but the message is accurate. You need to think about what expectations you are setting and ensure that these are met. This is true whether they are rises or falls.

Investors do not welcome a series of inaccurate and overestimated disclosures that fail to reflect actual performance. Chief executives have been sacked for less.

Given these demands, many organizations use a dedicated investor relations firm. However, these tend to address primarily institutional investors.

All that we have said so far about thinking from the position of the customer and the staff also applies here.

Questions

Are you complying with the statutory requirements?

What groups of investors are out there?

Who manages your investor relations?

Are you ensuring equal access for all groups?

Are you presenting your strategy without transgressing limitations of forward looking statements?

Are your statements acceptable within the regulatory provisions under which you are working?

In an international company, are you complying with requirements from other countries in which you are working?

---

7   International Financial Reporting Standards (IFRS) are a set of accounting standards. Currently they are issued by the International Accounting Standards Board (IASB). Many of the standards forming part of IFRS are known by the older name of International Accounting Standards (IAS).

8   The Sarbanes-Oxley Act of 2002 states that it is designed to 'to protect investors by improving the accuracy and reliability of corporate disclosure made pursuant to the securities law, and for other purposes.' See http://frwebgate.access.gpo.gov/cgi-bin/getdoc.cgi?dbname=107_cong_public_laws&docid=f:publ204.107.pdf.

REGULATORY BODIES

All industries have to comply with national and/or international financial reporting requirements depending upon the reporting regime they come under. Your accounting bodies will determine these, and you should check with your experts that statements are acceptable within the accounting provisions you are working under.

Similarly, in regulated industries, you may have to deal with specific regulatory bodies. These may have specific requirements that request information beyond that required for general disclosure. Examples would include financial services, some utilities and pharmaceuticals, depending upon the regulatory regime and country in which you are working.

Regulatory bodies require a level of compliance that you must reach as a minimum. You should also ensure that you comply with the spirit, as well as the letter, of the legislation.

Questions

What are the limitations on disclosure imposed by your regulators?

What additional information is required?

Who are your experts? Have you checked with them?

POLITICAL AND PRESSURE GROUPS

Consider the political implications of your announcements. These might be at local, national or international level depending upon your organization and the impact of the changes. You will have local and national politicians who may be interested in the success of your organization or its contribution and effect on the economy and their constituents. You can choose to involve politicians, or they may choose to involve themselves. In either case, you will need to actively manage that conversation and relationship.

If you are dealing with pressure groups, you need to understand which ones exist and choose how you want to respond to them.

Some organizations use political lobby groups to influence these pressure groups. They provide information in both directions: what are the politicians thinking and how do we influence them? It is valuable to think through how to respond to these groups, but there is another perspective:

> *'Organizations responding to pressure groups and stakeholders are weak managers doing so in the absence of a strong strategy.'*[9]

---

9   Look at the 'OECD risk management tool for investors in weak governance zones' for a more general assessment of how weak public and private sector governance affects investment risk:

You may think this is an extreme view, but it contains an important truth. Just because a group wishes to influence your organization or just because they are affected, you don't have to involve them in the thinking, inform them or accommodate their wishes. The opposite may be true. You might want to ignore them, brief against them or refuse to deal with them. The important point is to ensure you consider any pressure groups and choose your response to them.

Questions

What political or pressure groups are out there?

Which of these could you use to your purpose?

Which of these might others be using against you?

83

CONCLUSION

In this chapter you have been invited to think through how your strategy will be received from the perspective of other people. This 'second position' approach allows you to think through issues 'as if you were them'. It is no substitute for actually being them, but does provide insights into how other people think. Personally, I find it also exposes gaps and assumptions in my thinking.

Whether you are dealing with your staff directly, or through worker representation, they deserve the chance to be consulted and involved in the strategy. Similarly, customers and suppliers, particularly the bigger and more important ones who depend upon you or with whom you have a close working relationship, also deserve due consideration. Like unions, there may be statutory obligations to fulfil in the communication with investors and regulatory bodies.

We will now turn our attention to the strategy itself. We will explore what the strategy is that you want to communicate and the story of that strategy. How do we tell that story most effectively, to engage hearts, minds and hands?

November 2005, draft for consultation, www.oecdwatch.org/docs/OECD%20Risk%20Management%20Tool.pdf.

6   Developing the Story of the Strategy

We have explored with whom we want to communicate and the reactions we want. We have also explored the quality of the channels we have available and when best to start the communication. We now need to ensure that there is alignment and integrity over how the message is communicated.

This chapter helps you to develop the message of the strategy to ensure that it is coherent and has direction. In the following chapters, we will build its completeness and integrity, developing the method of how to tell it and how to ensure it is understood completely. First, we have to decide what the message is and how to articulate it.

So what is in the story? The basic elements are straightforward:

- Where are we now?

- Where do we want to go?

- How will we get there?

- Why will it be different this time?

- What is in it for me/you/them?

In telling the story, it is important to understand and match the thinking of the organization and to develop the elements of the story. These should include: Why should we leave? What are the first steps? What will be different? What's in it for me and for them? What are the financial implications, personally and organizationally? Strategy is about choice, so it is important to explain what you will do and also what you will not do. Often, the decision to stop doing something is as important as starting to do something or doing something better.

If strategy were easy, it would not be so interesting. Inherent in every strategy are tensions and sometimes apparent contradictions. These need to be made explicit as the story of the strategy is developed. Admitting the tensions and contradictions, for instance, expecting to do more with fewer people, will help its understanding.

In many organizations, there have been many waves of (often unsuccessful) change. You need to help people understand what will be different this time – why this time will be a success.

Some strategy and mission statements are simply words. It is more useful to have explicit and quantified targets for the future. People will want to know what the changes mean financially. They will also want to know how they will get there and what will be different. This chapter introduces the trap of 'strategy by hope and magic' so that you do not fall into it. Instead, you need to be explicit about what will cause change to happen in the organization.

'TOMORROW': CREATING A COMPELLING FUTURE

Having established where you are now, what is wrong and why changes need to be made, it is also necessary to be clear where you are going. You will also need to get the message across about why and how you are going there.

There are some common methods for doing this, including using mission and vision statements. We will cover these because they are popular. We will also cover their shortcomings and ways to overcome the shortcomings.

If you can describe the future in a more convincing way, it will build naturally on a mission or vision statement. Doing this makes the future become more real so it can be explained in a more compelling way beyond the mission statement.

VISION AND MISSION STATEMENTS

Just as the word 'strategy' has so many different meanings, the words 'mission' and 'vision' are both overused and subject to almost as many different definitions as there are people who want to define them. Collins and Porras[1] described 'vision' as one of the most overused and least understood words in the language.

Yet every organization has some sort of mission or vision statement: What sort of organization do we think we are? How do we identify ourselves? One way to think about this is, 'What are we also a part of?'

---

1   Collins, J. and Porras, G. (1999), *Built to Last: The Successful Habits of Visionary Companies*, 2nd edn (London: Random House Business Books).

Mission statements were often used as a way of making a more explicit change in the identity of the organization. This was very popular as an approach to strategic repositioning in the 1970s and 80s. Organizations that were mining aggregates could see themselves as part of the overall group of mining companies, part of the road surfacing and maintenance industry, or even a part of earth's resource utilization and replenishment.

Using their mission statement, they changed the way they described themselves from 'a mining company' to a 'manager and protector of the earth's resources'.

Questions

Write down (assuming your organization has them):

- *your mission statement*

- *your vision statement*

- *your organizational values*

What does your organization regard itself as a part of? Has the new strategy changed that? If so, how?

The challenge, when communicating the strategy in terms of vision and mission statements, is making it understandable; giving the statements meaning and, ideally the same meaning, to everyone.

In some organizations, when you ask about the corporate vision or mission, you are given a single statement. Sometimes it is as much as a page. There is a problem though: the short phrase can mean everything, and yet, at the same time, it can mean nothing. On one hand, everyone can agree it is desirable. On the other, it gives few clues about what to do about it and how to behave as a result.

It is the same if I ask you to think of a dog. (Go on, think of one now.) It is unlikely you are thinking of the same kind as I am. When first asked this question I thought of being attacked by a dog whilst out running. Everyone else in the room was thinking of particular dogs. There were labradors, alsatians, spaniels, puppies, mongrels and poodles. One person thought of the mess that dogs create on pavements.

The problem is that 'dog' is a nominalization here. 'Dog' is not a thing; it is a category of things. It is a concept. We know they have four legs and fur, and that they bark, but apart from that, they are quite different. There is no such thing as a generic dog. In two cases above we even had the effect of dogs rather than dogs themselves. The challenge when communicating such 'nominalizations' is to make it clear what they mean and how they are carried out.

Similarly, there is no such thing as generic 'excellent customer service'. We are clear when we meet examples of bad customer service (I'm sure you have a few you can bring to mind). There are basic standards that you expect. But there are also lots of different ways of delivering excellent customer service (and not all of them involve leaving a chocolate on your pillow).

Avis, for example, wanted to be number one in the car rental market that Hertz dominated. They are, but only through their subsidiary, Budget Rent-a-Car. Avis is now number three. So, there are lots of ways to be number one – including doing so as someone else. Budget represents economical rental. Avis represents a premium service. It would be interesting to compare which offers the best return on capital.

Why does this problem with mission statements becoming nominalizations occur? Well, if you have had a period of reflection, or a lengthy workshop or management away-day to develop your mission and vision, it is possible that you discussed several thousand words as a management team. You shared ideas, provided examples, discussed exceptions, articulated futures, stated desires and expressed strong feelings about what you wanted and how you felt you wanted to get there. At the end of the session, all this was distilled into about 20 to 30 words.

The problem is, the rest of the organization was not there. They were not privy to that extensive discussion. There is no way people can guess the rest that went on behind these 30 words. What 'trust' means to me is possibly quite different from what it means to you.

The responsibility of management, therefore, is to bring these statements to life. You cannot expect people to read a mission statement and necessarily understand it from your perspective, unless you can communicate how you feel. For this reason, many organizations also rely on core values to guide people's activities and behaviours. They add the standards of behaviour that are expected alongside the direction and purpose.

Questions

Revisit your mission and vision statements:

- *What detail do you have behind them?*
- *How do you get past the nominalizations?*
- *How do you explain them and tell the stories behind them?*
- *What makes them real?*
- *How do you live by them?*

One way to address this problem is to break down the 'vision' into component parts. In *Built to Last*, Collins and Porras suggest that it contain two components: a core ideology and an envisioned future.

The core ideology should consist of a clear set of core values that represent the organization's enduring tenets. These tenets are a small set of guiding principles that require no external justification, but have an intrinsic importance inside the organization. They are also personal to the organization. For example, they described Proctor and Gamble as, 'Not treating product excellence as a strategy for success. They treated it as an almost religious tenet for over five decades helped by P&G people.'

This core value would be accompanied by a core purpose. For instance, 3M use, 'To solve unsolved problems, innovatively.' Walt Disney describe their core purpose as, 'To make people happy.'

The two authors also suggest that the organization needs an 'envisioned future' as a part of its vision. In part, this should consist of a BHAG ('Big Hairy Audacious Goal')[2] and in part a vivid description of the future. They suggest a BHAG should be a goal for the whole organization that spans 10 to 30 years. They suggest that just trying to create such a goal forces the management team to be visionary.

Questions

What is your organization's 'core ideology'?

- *Its core values?*
- *Its core purpose?*

What is your organization's BHAG?

I have come across only a few organizations with BHAGs. Unfortunately, most of those organizations came from the dot.com era and have perished long before their BHAGs were achieved.

However, the second part of the 'envisioned future', a vivid and explicit description of the future, is both much more valuable to the management team and much more enduring. Having worked to develop them as a consultant to organizations for between 5 and 10 years now, I know of several whose visions have come to fruition or are still in use.

How is this persistency and usefulness achieved?

---

2   There are other suggestions as to what BHAG stands for.

DESCRIBING A COMPELLING FUTURE

How do you make the vision of the future more tangible and explicit? A powerful way is to articulate it 'as if you *are* there'. The effect of doing this well, making the future tangible, is to make it understandable, easier to appreciate, and ultimately, compelling.

> *At a large retailer, the chief executive was complaining, 'They didn't get the strategy.'*
>
> *When we interviewed him, we asked him to pick a point in the future, say 3 or 5 years from now and to describe what his stores look and feel like.*
>
> *He chose 5 years hence, rolled back his head, closed his eyes and started talking. What followed was a detailed tour of a store from the customer's perspective. He started outside with what it looked like and walked inside and around the store. Twenty-five minutes later, our pens were practically smoking. This was the vision in his head that the others did not experience or share. We had asked only a few questions as prompts to clarify or add some detail.*
>
> *What we now had was a picture of the stores of the future, as if we were there.*

The key is to choose points in time and explore what they *are actually like* – to describe what you see, hear and feel. Then move on to the same aspects at a different point in time and explore what it is like, then, as if you are there also.

When you describe the future in this way it becomes more real; more real for you and more real for those you describe it to. When most people describe the future, they describe what it *will be* like. We are describing what it *is* like. This is a subtle but important difference.

Whenever I do this with clients I find three effects. First, they describe the future in a way that, perhaps even to themselves, they had not articulated as clearly or in as much detail as they have before. If you ask for detail, you will also get it.

> *Whilst I was working with a city council, the council's management team wanted to develop a university in the city. It was a project that was not going anywhere.*
>
> *So we picked a point when it would be established and then asked some details. How many students? Where did they come from? Where was it situated? What subjects? How did it contribute to the community? What was the effect on the economy and how did it relate to local business?*
>
> *Oddly enough, none of the directors had described this before to one another in such detail. It was just 'the university'.*

By making it real, they could see that the current approach of letting the local college develop into a university was not going to work. Two years later, detailed plans were afoot to establish the university.

Second, most clients forget about the problems they have today and the obstacles along the way. They are talking as if these have been overcome. Moreover, if you ask them how they overcame them, they will tell you. In contrast, if you ask what will happen and then ask what needs to be overcome they will tell you about the problems they still face and have not yet overcome. They often describe some remaining problems that are so large that they restrict the ability to see the future picture.

Third, it makes for a much richer discussion about the future amongst the directors. Instead of talking about the subject, say, the university, as some generic object, they talk about specifics. The discussion moves from a dog to that cute little golden retriever puppy.

Questions

Pick an aspect of your strategy for which you want to articulate a future.

Pick a point in time in the future

Describe what you want it to be like.

Describe what it is like, as if you are there.

- *What do you see?*

- *What do you feel?*

- *What do you hear?*

- *Who else is there?*

- *What are you doing?*

- *What is the organization like now?*

- *What are your customers saying, doing, feeling?*

- *What are your staff, saying, doing, feeling?*

- *What else do you notice?*

Pick different points in time. How do these affect things?

One of the interesting aspects of this approach is that you can describe unattractive or uncertain futures, as well:

'Imagine what happens if we continue along the path we are taking. By 2010 we are in a situation where our customers are leaving us and we will have had to make half the workforce redundant ...'

In the same way, by making it real, you are creating a compelling future (in this case undesirable). You are communicating it in a way that becomes real for people.

For the mission and vision statements, this approach puts detail into the words. If you do want to become the number one in the industry, you can describe what number one means: number one in what respect? Is it in turnover, profitability, volume of sales, most popular with a particular customer group, or what?

It is not enough for the managing director or chief executive to believe in the objective, target or vision of the future. The management challenge is to convince everyone in the board room, and then the rest of the organization, that this is both attractive and achievable. This becomes more important the greater the stretch involved. It is easy to agree modest targets for change.

The real management challenge is getting the team to agree ambitious targets for change, and getting them to believe that they can achieve them, so they can convince others that they are achievable.

Questions

How ambitious are your objectives?

Who believes in them? To what extent are they believed?

What needs to be done to ensure that the whole management team believe that these ambitious targets are credible and achievable?

Can they convince others that they are credible and achievable as well as ambitious?

WHAT YOU WILL DO AND WHAT YOU WON'T DO

Michael Porter, the well-known writer on strategy, said, 'Competitive advantage is at the heart of any strategy, and achieving competitive advantage requires a firm to make a choice…about the competitive advantage it seeks to attain and the scope within which to attain it.'[3] So strategy is about what you choose to do and also what not to do. Often a change in strategy involves stopping doing something. If you want to be slim, it is about not going to the fridge, as well as taking more exercise.

The message of the strategy should indicate where and when different aspects of the strategy apply. Does the strategy apply to all offices and regions, nationally and/or internationally? When will it start and will it roll out at the same time? When and where does it not apply?

---

3   Porter, M.E. (1985), *Competitive Advantage: Creating and Sustaining Competitive Performance* (New York: Free Press), p. 12.

Make sure you communicate these points.

Remember that strategy is often reflected in a pattern of behaviour. You need to put in place ways to discourage the old pattern of behaviour as well as encourage the new. What will now discourage you from doing this? Communicate these as well.

Perhaps you might cut off budgets, switch off old systems, reallocate people and resources, or withdraw products or services. Perhaps you will no longer serve unprofitable customers in the same way. If there are too many suppliers, perhaps you will stop using some sources.

> *The chief executive of a service company wanted to destroy the old culture of rules and poor customer service. He wanted to encourage customer service people to think about what customer service really meant. He made a clear statement: 'Imagine that it is your mother or grandmother on the end of the phone. Now what would you do to ensure that she got appropriate service?'.*
>
> *The message was simple: no more hand-offs to other people. Find new boundaries, and we will rein in the more extreme cases, rather than applying unnecessary rules to everyone.*

This message not only gave a call for action but established a new level of trust. Such moves often send strong signals to both the people who operate the system and those it affects: this is what we will stop doing, and this is how we will stop you doing it. Explain why.

Questions

What things do you have to stop doing to make sure your strategy will be successful?

What do you have to put in place to discourage people from doing this anymore?

Who needs to make these changes? How will you explain these changes to them?

Who does it also affect? Have you explained to them as well?

FUTURE TARGETS

One popular way to express where you want to be is by setting targets. Some organizations build these into their vision statements. For others, it is better to have a rallying call for the mission statement and a more specific statement with a target for where they want to be in the next 2, 3 or 5 years.

For instance, we will:

- have doubled turnover within 3 years;
- have increased profitability by 30 per cent;

- have increased total shareholder return within 5 years;

- have moved to number one in the market within 4 years;

- be the largest exporter of this product by in 3 years time;

- increase our ROI to 15 per cent in 3 years time.

These sort of statements communicate a simple, clear message: we will achieve this high level figure.

Quite often these figures are tied to board and executive remuneration. Sometimes they are tied to the overall bonus for all employees.

The big question in most people's minds is, 'What does it specifically mean to me?' or 'How can I possibly affect that?' The answer is to ensure that people have a clear line of sight from what they influence, to the target.

For instance, if an increase in profitability is the target, people can target revenue volume, margin on sales, cost of sales, operational costs or fixed costs.

When relative performance is used, it becomes harder to assess the level of performance needed. For instance, how many others in the industry are also aiming to be 'Number One'? How do you know what a competitor is doing in customer service, so you can be better? In the example below, this company has chosen its performance relative to stock market returns.

An established retailer had been set a target by its group board to increase its Total Shareholder Return (TSR)[4] by 25 per cent over the next 5 years.

When we explored this with the board, we realized this was accepted as a given by seven of the team, but two regarded it as unachievable. One of the two was the finance director.

He believed there were two aspects that made it an unrealistic target. First, market share price movements outside their control would have a larger influence on total return to shareholders (share price plus dividends) than they could influence. Secondly, putting share price volatility aside, as an established retailer, they would have to generate a dramatic change to either volume of sales, or margin on sales, to achieve this sort of return. This was at a time of increasing share price pressures.

In essence, most of the board accepted the target they were given, but chose to either ignore how unrealistic it was, or were not aware of it. The finance director regarded it as an unrealistic target that he could not argue with, because it came from the group board.

---

4   TSR, Total Shareholder Return, is the total of the increase in share price and the dividends distributed to shareholders.

Either way, the implications were not understood and it was very unlikely it was going to be achieved.

The whole situation with this organization was exacerbated by a team of financial consultants who analyzed all the numbers for the chief executive. Their role was to vet the financial viability of any projects. Thus, managers making proposals felt separated from the target they were being incentivized to achieve.

This is an extreme example. There are many where a clear message has got through, based upon a clear target, backed up with thorough training.

A large manufacturing company was not managing its cash. They realized that there was little appreciation of the cash implications of decisions that managers were making. So they not only put in place clear cash generation targets for their staff with incentives, they also embarked on an extensive cash management training regime.

Every senior manager was trained to understand the cash implications of the decisions they made. Thus, the implications of offering different terms on contracts, late payers, cutting margins on products and investments, were more fully understood.

The initial training was followed up with support from finance to help the managers apply the techniques they learnt on the courses (and compensate for some financial illiteracy). Within 18 months they had turned the cash position around.

Not only did the strategy involve a high-level target, it was backed up with training and support, so that the managers could appreciate and understand better the decisions they were making.

One advantage of this 'compelling future' approach is that it also serves to quantify such numbers as well as put them in a context. For example, if the organization is to increase its margins and cash flow over the next 3 years, these are the other targets we need to be hitting in years one and two and also the other 'enablers' that need to be in place and working well to make them happen.

Questions

What high-level targets does your strategy have?

Are the implications of them understood?

What other things need to be put in place to put these targets in people's 'line of sight'?

How can you make these targets meaningful and relevant to decision makers on a day-to-day basis?

WHAT DOES IT MEAN FINANCIALLY?

When explaining the strategy it is important to explain the economic model: 'How will it make us money?', 'How will this make us more profitable?', 'How will this increase revenue?' and 'How will this reduce costs?'

These are likely to be expressed in terms such as:

- This is our turnover, market size, capacity and costs now, and this is where we want to be in the future.

- This is how we will change our cost base, or increase our margin.

- This is how we will get more revenue per customer or perhaps change the customers to ones that are more valuable.

- These are the new customers for our products, and this is what we will be selling.

These statements are even valid for non-profit organizations. A charity needs to know where its income stream is coming from. A city council needs to know what funding it will receive from its grants and tax revenues. A hospital needs to know what income will be generated per patient or per procedure.

At the same time, cost models will be changing. The strategy will affect the operational costs of the business. By outsourcing we will reduce our costs by *x* per cent, or by increasing the volume of sales we will better use our fixed assets. We will change our sales model, so more customers come to us via the Internet and therefore reduce the cost of sales.

Any strategy is likely to involve a cost of change. This might be associated with projects or programmes of work aimed at delivering a better process, the cost of redundancy or investment in a new factory.

There will also be risk. In most organizations there are commercial risks. In some there are risks associated with compliance or statutory requirements.

What is important is to engage people in the economics of the business. The level of detail need not (and should not) include all the detailed financial calculations but should explain the broad economics. Remember Heresy 1 (Chapter 2): People are not stupid. For example:

1. 'At the moment we make this much per car and we want to be making this much. Steel prices have risen by 40 per cent which has cut our margins from 8 per cent to 4 per cent.'

2. 'If we can avoid an increase in costs above inflation, whilst managing the eroding prices, we will remain profitable.'

When people understand how what they do affects the costs, they are better positioned to make informed judgements about helping to improve it. If they are kept away from the economics, how can they understand and assist?

Questions

What is your economic model for the business?

What are the economic levers or drivers of your strategy?

Can you explain these in a simple expression?

HOW WILL WE GET THERE?

In the remainder of this chapter we explore the following simple question: if our strategy says, 'This is where we are' and 'This is where we want to go,' the remaining question is, 'How will we get there?'

Then we explore what actually creates the change in strategy. We will also highlight strategies that have no drivers of change: 'strategy by hope and magic'. You will also find a checklist to make sure you know what combination of things might be driving your strategy and change.

Developing this theme further, we look at cause and effect in the strategy. We provide a simple model with four steps that enables you to explain how the underlying capabilities, culture, skills and knowledge will change the financial results and the customer experience.

Next we explore one particular aspect that drives change: organizational values. In many organizations these play a crucial role. In others they merely sit on the wall in a picture frame. They are given special mention because you will need congruence between your strategy and your organizational values to be convincing.

Finally we look at cultural inertia and scepticism as well as the innate contradictions or tensions that exist within any strategy.

STRATEGY BY HOPE AND MAGIC

A venture capitalist once described to me how he had seen a recent business plan that included developing new business in Europe, with up to 25 per cent of the revenue in 3 years time coming from exports.

However, when he looked at the skills of the management team, there were no international marketing skills. There was no experience of setting up distributor networks or sales teams abroad. There was no analysis of the overseas markets. There was no investment in the business to pay for the overseas sales, no expenses, no overseas advertising or promotion, no training, no costs, no support. Somehow these sales from overseas were just going to materialize.

I call this 'strategy by hope and magic'.

'Somehow we will be different, but we are not going to explain how.' I have seen this in a far simpler form. We will be 10 per cent more efficient next year, or we will have cut costs by 15 per cent, or we will have 20 per cent more happier customers, but nothing is changing. It is as if the mere act of saying we will change will bring it about.

To some extent this is true. The Hawthorne experiments in the 1920s showed that factory productivity increased when the lights were actually turned up or when they pretended to turn them up. Productivity increased simply because more interest and attention was paid to the workers.

To some extent, simply focusing peoples' attention on things will generate change. This strategy is one that is often used in central government in the UK. By stating what will be measured (and setting targets) they hope that things will improve. The trouble is, this form of change is not necessarily sustainable, nor controllable. Moreover, too many targets simply create confusion. You can't focus on everything.

Table 6.1 lists over 30 potential drivers of change. It is not an exhaustive list. Nor is it a list of strategic options. It is an example of the drivers of change internally. There are many things that can be done to improve performance and execute a strategy. These are just some of them. The question is, what combinations are you using?

Questions

What is changing?

Why is it changing? What is going to cause your strategy and organization to change?

What combination of things are you using to create these changes?

What will drive your strategy? What will make it happen?

How explicit have you made this?

Table 6.1   Drivers of change

• Investment in people	• Better analysis of information
• Investment in processes	• Improving marketing
• New technology	• Strengthening networks
• Changing incentives	• Strengthening relationships
• Changing management	• Greater understanding of your
• Changed motivation	customers
• Better communication	• Improving personal objectives
• Increased skills	• Stopping doing things
• Increased knowledge	• Greater supplier relations
• Changed behaviours	• Lowering supplier costs
• Applying measures	• Lowering operational costs
• Setting targets	• Making responsibility clearer
• Raising targets	• Changing culture
• Introducing new products or	• Emphasizing the organizational
services	values
• Removing old products or	• Financial re-engineering
services	• Improving delegation and
• Increasing understanding	empowerment

ORGANIZATIONAL VALUES

In some organizations the values are in a picture frame on the wall. In other organizations you don't need a plaque on the wall, for they are being lived and acted out continuously. You don't need reminders.

You can't actually see a 'value'. These values are the criteria by which we judge things, make decisions and behave. You can see behaviours associated with values. For instance, you don't see 'respect for the customer and staff', but you will see people being respectful and showing respect. You may also see people being disrespectful to the client or an individual. Showing disrespect is an action or behaviour; an employee has crossed the boundary of what is acceptable behaviour.

Personal values and ethics influence our lives, behaviours and actions. We have many values, though most of the time we don't notice them, because they are so innate to our ways of thinking and working. However, if someone is disrespectful of our values, or acts in a way that is contrary to them, we tend to notice very quickly. There is generally a quite noticeable and strong reaction.

Our personal values often appear as the voice in our heads that tells us that this or that is the right thing to do, or the reaction in our stomachs that tells us that someone's behaviour is not appropriate.

The set of values of an organization is the collective, implicitly agreed set of values by which the people in the organization are operating. Organizational values are the collective voices of conscience and the collective gut instinct, in the people within the organization.

Whilst we have many values as individuals, most organizations distil their stated organizational values down to six or so. This small set of organizational values acts as a rallying call and the values are chosen to influence behaviour. They are also used to establish clear boundaries that should not be crossed. There can be a disconnection between the values in operation and the stated values.

Some organizations just use individual words, or very short phrases, to denote their values: trust, service, respect, integrity, value. These phrases leave huge space for personal interpretation. What 'trust', 'service' or 'respect' mean to you or me may be very different than for other people. To counter this, other organizations include both the words and an explanation of their characteristics. They seek phrases that encourage and clarify the action associated with the values. A particularly effective example of this is, 'Hire the best, and trust them.' It says so much about what to do in so few words. It makes an explicit statement and call to action.

You can also communicate values through stories, actions, how you behave, what you do, how you judge things, what you say, who you recruit, how you recruit, who you promote, who you sack.

The crucial point is that your words and your behaviour need to be consistent if you are to communicate coherent values. If you say, 'I will trust you, but I'll be back down tomorrow to check on how you are getting on,' is that a consistent message of trust? Or has the trust been undermined by the return the next day?

Remember the heresies from Chapter 2. A key theme of these involved trust, respect and assuming your people are intelligent human beings. If you espouse trust but then don't act on it, clearly this is not a value that you will communicate. 'How do you communicate values in an organization?' The answer is, through consistency of words and actions. Actions need to be consistent with the values you espouse. You have to act, not as if they were true, *but because they are true.*

Questions

What are your organizational values, according to your literature?

What are the values that people act out and talk about?

How does the strategy integrate the organization's values?

What actions will you take in communicating the strategy to emphasize the values?

CAUSE AND EFFECT

I regularly come up against organizations that are having trouble explaining how changes associated with their strategy will ripple through to the bottom line. They are often missing a coherent story of how one component of the strategy affects other parts to make the whole strategy happen. One way to tell the story and track the impact of the change is to do it through a cause and effect model.

Let us take an example. Commercial organizations will have an overall objective or vision that will rely on them making money. They make money because their customers pay them for a satisfactory product or service (and they produce the goods or services at an economic cost). The organization will undertake many activities to satisfy customer needs. These will rely on various elements of behaviours, skills, knowledge and infrastructure. As we have seen, these underlying capabilities will be influenced by the organization's values.

So, if we can influence the values, improve the skills, knowledge and capabilities, the organization will develop so that its processes improve, it will produce better products, more economically, which will satisfy its customers even more, so it can make more profits and achieve its overall purpose.

This cause and effect model of the performance of an organization is shown in Figure 6.1.

Figure 6.2 shows part of the cause and effect chain for an organization using this structure. From the top, this shows that the organization believes it can improve its margin, by both growing turnover and having a lower cost of sales. From the customer's perspective, the organization believes that its clients want a specialist they can trust and higher quality bids. Presumably the customers are also incurring unnecessary bid costs. To deliver these benefits for its customers, the organization believes it should focus on having better quality leads and bidding for the right business. The organization believes it needs to better prove its capability and develop the quality of its contacts. Finally, its thinking is underpinned by two core values: quality and a culture of innovation. These influence how it thinks about its strategy and represent behaviours that it wants to encourage.

You can also read the cause and effect picture from the bottom. Product quality and innovation drive their ability to improve the quality of its contacts and proving its capability, they will get better quality leads and be better at bidding for the right business, so that their customers will know they have a specialist they can trust and make better quality bids, which will lead to turnover growth, lower cost of sales and improved margins.

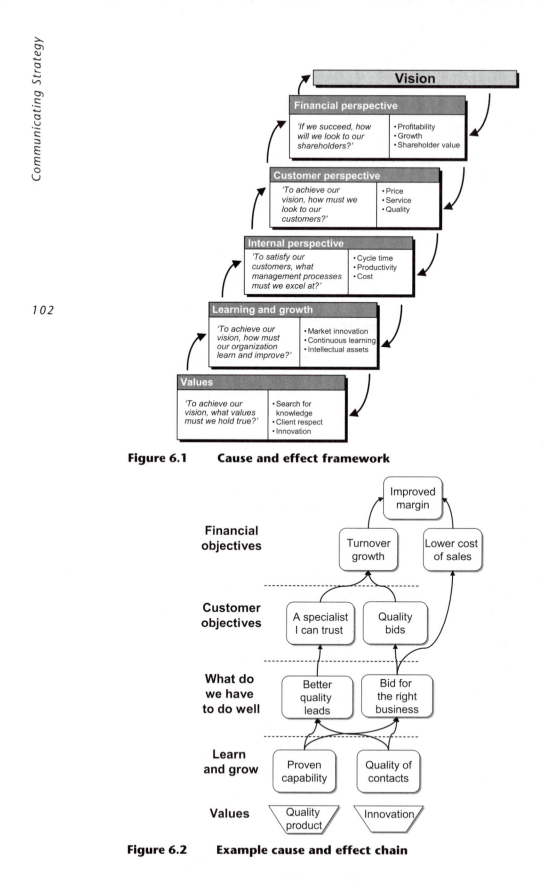

Figure 6.1   Cause and effect framework

Figure 6.2   Example cause and effect chain

NEW BEHAVIOURS, SKILLS AND CAPABILITIES

Writing the strategy with causes and effects, as a strategy map, can be revealing. You need to ask: 'What behaviours will change? What specific actions should we take and what should we not do? What behaviours are we trying to encourage? What behaviours are we trying to discourage?'

Whilst working with one organization I tried mapping their strategy from the corporate plan. As well as making 5 per cent cost savings, service was going to improve. The hard part was working out how. It became apparent that there were almost no references to changes in behaviour, culture, skills, knowledge and technology that would make a change. The entire perspective of learning and growth capabilities was missing. I am sure someone, somewhere, had thought about it, but it was not clear from the strategy document.

There were many actions and a few projects that might have brought about some change, but they did not look substantial enough to make the major changes required (and there were no costs for either carrying them out, or managing the consequences of them). Simply by casting the strategy as a cause and effect picture we had highlighted a major issue with their strategy. It appeared to be strategy by 'hope and magic' with nothing changing their behaviours.

Often an improvement in a process is expected, but it is not clear what will change it. This is one reason why IT systems and business process re-engineering often fail. The new systems are put in and people are expected to change their behaviours, but they don't know how to or why. Likewise, changing the process without providing new skills won't fundamentally change what is going on.

If your strategy requires a change in behaviour, but fails to explain how you will bring it about, or encourage that change in behaviour, you will have great difficulty sustaining it. However, if you start to change the skills, knowledge and capabilities of people, you give them new resources to change their behaviours.

Questions

What new skills, knowledge and capabilities do we need to develop?

How are these different from the skills and capabilities we used to have?

How will these be acquired?

PUTTING ALL THE PIECES INTO A STRATEGY MAP

You may have realized that the cause and effect model just described is actually the structure of a strategy map.[5] In fact all the components for telling

103

---

5   Norton, D.P. and Kaplan, R.S. (2001), *The Strategy Focused Organization* (Boston, Massachusetts: Harvard Business School Press).

the story of the strategy that have been described in the last two chapters go towards building a strategy map that can be used to tell the story of the strategy. The single cause and effect chain in the example in Figure 6.2 is just one part of the organization's strategy. Once the whole strategy is mapped this way, you get a strategy map for the organization. This technique is called strategy mapping.

A strategy map is a one-page picture of the strategy that you can use to tell the story of the strategy of your organization. Strategy maps were developed alongside balanced scorecards when it was realized that tables of measures and targets were very poor at describing a strategy. Whereas the scorecard captures the various measures in perspectives, the strategy map shows pictorially the relationships between the objectives that are being measured and how delivering these objectives (and targets) will make the strategy happen. So strategy mapping is the part of a modern balanced scorecard approach that helps to explain and communicate the strategy.

Let us relate the elements of the strategy map to the discussions so far. At the beginning of this chapter we established a vision or mission for the organization.[6] A summary of this is placed at the top of the strategy map and if you have developed a rich picture of the compelling vision of the future, as it will be, you can have this as a supporting picture.

We established what the strategy meant financially, so the main financial objectives are placed beneath this purpose or vision statement because they directly contribute to it. The customers provide the money and, therefore, the customer objectives are placed beneath the financials and linked to them. These customer objectives come from the 'What's in it for me' thinking from the customer's perspective you did earlier.

The choice of what you put in the process perspective will depend upon how you choose to satisfy your customers' needs. You want to avoid strategy by hope and magic, so the underlying capabilities, skills, knowledge and drivers of change will be placed in the learning and growth perspective. Finally the organization's values underpin the capabilities.

The strategy map should include a cause and effect model. The chains of cause and effect help you tell the story of the strategy, explain how you will get there and, as we have seen, also help you to avoid the 'strategy by hope and magic' syndrome from which some organizations suffer.

Of course the strategy map is not the whole story. There will be a financial model that describes the strategy financially. There will be additional words that describe the objectives and put flesh on the bones of the picture. There will be measures and targets for the objectives. When the story is told there

---

6   This approach is specifically for commercial organizations. A slightly different structure is used for public sector and not-for-profit organizations.

will be the passion, emotion and commitment of the management team who are telling the story so people can see, hear and read about the strategy. As we shall see in the next chapter, this combination of ways of telling the story of the strategy makes it clear and gets the whole message across for a wide variety of people.

Figure 6.3 shows a more extensive strategy map from an engineering contractor. Again, this is a simplified extract, but you can see by reading it in the same way, from top to bottom, that it tells a story of improving its growth and project delivery by improving its procurement, alliances, commercial skills, and technical and project management capability.

Notice how the customer perspective describes what the customers want from their point of view: a proven capability, the best price/cost solution and on time, on cost quality. In contrast, the process perspective describes what the engineering contractor needs to do well to deliver this: demonstrate its capability in the bid process and excellent project delivery.

As is common with these diagrams, the learning and growth perspective provides a key to the capabilities that the organization needs to develop. As it develops these capabilities, it expects that it will improve its ability to bid well and deliver projects, which ultimately leads to happier customers and improved financial results.

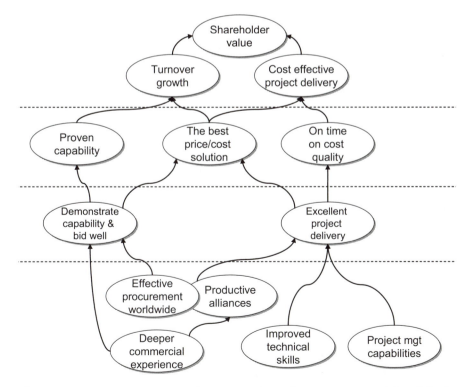

Figure 6.3   Strategy map for an engineering contractor (simplified)

This approach also works just as well in public sector and not-for-profit organizations. Figure 6.4 shows part of a strategy map from a city council. This strategy map is based upon work at a city council, which is one of the top environmental cities in the UK. It represents part of the environmental services and planning department's strategy map, though it has moved on since this version was developed.

To create an attractive and environmentally friendly city it needs to satisfy the needs of three stakeholders. Residents want a clean place to live and work that also protects the environment for future generations. Private sector developers will work with the city council to grow the city: as commercial organizations they want to make money as well as have support for their developments from the city council, otherwise they will go elsewhere. Development agencies and politicians want to see sustainable growth.

These 'customers' do not give money in the same way as a commercial organization, but they do expect the city council to operate a cost effective service and support economic growth and prosperity.

To do all this well, the council needs to ensure it provides sustainable transport services as well as cost effective waste management and energy use. At the same time it needs to ensure it encourages economically sustainable developments whilst planning an integrated set of city developments.

The city council therefore needs to develop some underlying capabilities. These include having the right people and skills in place, building skills, knowledge and capability in sustainable development. They need to learn how to work effectively with the various partners and to attract inward investment, as well as engage the community behind the initiatives.

You can see that, in telling this story, it is clear where the city council will focus its attention. There are of course many other aspects to the strategy, in the detail of its implementation. However this strategy map, on a single page, provides a clear picture of how the council will help and support the development of a sustainable and environmental city.

These strategy map presentations are very powerful because they allow the presenter to both show and tell the story at the same time. Moreover, they do this in a very logical way, but also with passion and emotion, so people can hear it, see it and feel it.

Of course, these strategy maps are not the only way to show a strategy pictorially. However, my experience has been that the cause and effect structure of these maps means that a more thorough and systematic representation is developed and then told.

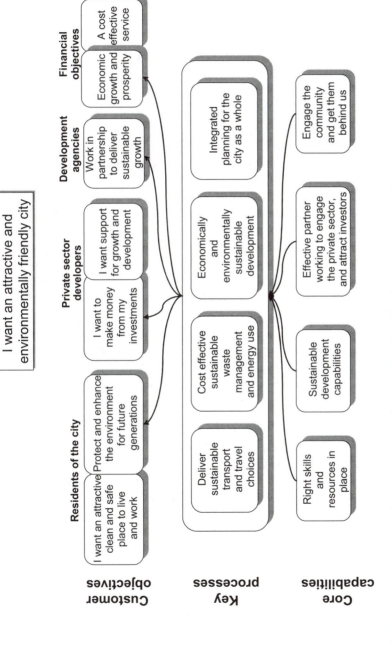

Figure 6.4   **Strategy map for a city council's sustainable development (extract)**

Questions

How would explaining your strategy as a strategy map help it to be understood?

What would the map of your strategy look like?

How clear are the cause and effect links that should drive the change and the strategy?

USING STRATEGY MAPS TO COMMUNICATE THE STRATEGY

Strategy maps provide a very effective way to communicate a complex strategy to a large number of people. With one client, we had a top level strategy map and six lower level ones owned by the various directors. The challenge was to engage the 50 or so key middle managers in the organization.

> *The chief executive and her directors presented their seven strategy maps. Each took roughly 5 to 10 minutes to tell the story from their map, before moving on to the next director. Within an hour, the executive team had told the whole story of their strategy. For the next 2 hours, the middle managers were let loose on A0 sized versions of the strategy maps and were invited to comment on them, ask questions and add their thoughts about where they could help to deliver the changes.*

> *The energy in the room was extremely high and the conversations, involving people from widely differing departments, were animated and enthusiastic. The chief executive described the event as the single most effective thing that was done to communicate the strategy and engage the middle managers' enthusiasm and ownership of the strategy.*

As one of the senior managers later put it, 'It was the first time that the executive team had communicated their strategy without resorting to a thick document.' Another manager said, 'Now I can carry the strategy around in my pocket. If I am unsure of someone's strategy, I can simply look at their strategy map and say, "can you explain this please?" That is so powerful.'

The strategy maps were so effective that, as a result of the work, the high-level corporate plan became just seven pages.

Questions

How do you intend to brief and engage your middle managers?

What could you gain by such an open discussion of your strategy?

How do they carry around and discuss, or clarify, the strategy at the moment?

ADMITTING TO TENSIONS AND CONTRADICTIONS

Every strategy I have come across has some tension and contradiction within it, somewhere. For example:

- growth, with profitability;

- increasing sales whilst reducing costs;

- managing costs and quality and timely delivery on a project;

- maximizing factory utilization and capacity whilst minimizing inventory and stock;

- developing and introducing new products whilst still having the cash cows of existing products;

- getting customers to upgrade their technology quickly, whilst risking the frustration of built-in redundancy and having to support too many products;

- changing the profile to more profitable customers, without 'throwing the baby out with the bath water';

- narrowing down the supplier lists without raising prices.

Frankly, if I have not discovered the tensions in the strategy, I don't believe it. If it is that simple, and there are no tensions, then I probably don't understand it.

If you have not identified the tensions and contradictions, then your staff, customers, suppliers or investors will. So, admit to the contradictions. Be honest about the tensions and pressures that the strategy will create.

The picture of the strategy as a strategy map allows you to place the pieces that are creating the tension alongside one another, so you can explain how they fit together and how the natural tensions within the strategy are operating and need managing by your staff.

CONCLUSION

As you worked through this chapter you will have been developing your strategy and adding detail to the description of the strategy to make it richer. You will also have been practising how to communicate elements of your strategy story by adding more detail to that story.

By now you should have a clear picture of where you want to go, a definite idea of how you will get there, and have eliminated all the hope and magic. This picture will have been shared amongst your management team, so that they all have a consistent story.

The next step is to be able to tell that story in a consistent and compelling manner: to tell the story so that it engages people; to bring it to life for people so that it enters their heads, hands and hearts.

7 Let Me Tell You a Story

Having established our understanding of the strategy, we now move to telling the story of the strategy more effectively.

By the end of this chapter you will be a better storyteller. You will be able to tell the story of your strategy in a compelling manner that engages people. You will learn about the power of stories and how they are used in organizations to communicate its ethos. These stories are often metaphors for how the organization is changing. You will also understand the power of quotations, for as someone once said, 'A well chosen quote is worth a thousand words.'

Much of the power of these stories comes from how they are told. Good storytellers use language techniques to engage their audience. You will get a feel for what a good story sounds like.

Effective presentation starts by pacing the audience and then bringing them to where you want them to be. Without this it can be difficult to take a group with you. You will learn techniques that will allow you to pace your audience's thinking, so you can lead them towards where you want them to go. As you do this, the ideas that you have already developed from other chapters can be woven into your presentations.

As the chapter develops, you will build an understanding of the different ways that people think and how they are convinced in different ways. This understanding is used by powerful speakers to engage and touch large audiences. Using this method, you will start to develop your own style of engaging audiences and build a more compelling way of telling the story of your strategy.

THE VALUE OF STORIES

You have probably noticed that we have been telling stories throughout this book. Talk to any anthropologist and they will tell you that stories form a key part of almost any society. Many religious texts contain stories and parables. Stories get passed down as folklore within families, social groups and organizations. Just think about the stories you have heard of:

- Apple computing starting in a garage;

- IBM letting Microsoft provide their early operating system;

- how Virgin started with Richard Branson living on a boat;

- the birth of the 3M Post-it note.

I don't have to tell these stories, just mention them. Stories about organizations, and in organizations have resonance with the reader (or listener) for a reason.

> *When I first joined one particular (large blue chip) consultancy, there were stories about the senior partner. He had a reputation for causing male consultants (in a very macho organization) to leave his office crying. He was reputed to have said things like, 'Everyone is entitled to make a mistake, you have made yours!' or, 'Do you know where your next mortgage payment is coming from?'. He made it very clear that you were to be absolutely sure of your facts, conclusions and recommendations for a client: if not, you were taken apart.*

In contrast I often tell the story of being interviewed at another consultancy (which I am really pleased to say I did join).

> *The person interviewing me simply walked in, introduced himself as Steve, and started chatting. It felt like being interviewed by a peer consultant. It was only later that I was told he was the managing director. He really set the tone for the style of the organization. Grade did not matter. What mattered was the quality of your contribution. It was an immensely respectful organization, in quite a different way from other consultancies I worked for.*

These stories exist for a reason. They exist to pass on the characteristics of the organization; embed the culture of the organization; give clues about how to act; how to make judgements; and how to work together.

Many powerful stories involve the founders. Many others involve what customers are doing or want, or how they received exceptional service. They provide exemplars of good practice. Sometimes the stories are apocryphal or fictional, though if they are they have elements of truth.

Questions

What stories exist in your organization? Ask around to see what other people hear.

What messages do they give out?

What stories would be consistent with what you are trying to achieve?

There are two variations on stories that we will explore briefly: using metaphors and using quotations.

THE VALUE OF METAPHOR

Many years ago an old man was tending his crops when a knight came past. The knight hailed the man working in the fields and asked, 'Are you from around here?' 'Yes,' answered the man. 'Then tell me,' said the knight. 'What are the people like in that village further up the road?'

The old man thought for a while and said, 'Before I answer, tell me where have you come from?' 'I came from the village back there along the road,' replied the knight. 'And tell me, what were the people like in that village?' asked the old man.

The knight dropped his head, 'Oh dear, they were unfriendly and surly and inhospitable. I left as soon as I could.'

'Well,' replied the old man, 'I am afraid to say that the people in that village further along the road are very much the same.' 'Oh,' replied the knight and thanking the old man, off he rode.

Some months later, whilst the man was again tending his crops, another knight came along the same road from the same direction. Again, the knight stopped, hailed the old man and asked, 'Are you from around here?' Again, the man replied, 'Yes, I am.' The knight then asked, ' I would like to know what those people in the village further up the road are like.' The old man thought for a while and then asked, 'Where have you come from?' The knight mentioned the same village as the previous knight. 'And what were the people there like?' The old man asked.

The knight beamed. 'Oh, they were lovely, very hospitable and so friendly that, although I only planned to stay one night, I ended up staying for three.'

'Well,' replied the old man, 'I think you will find that the people in the village you are heading for are just as lovely, friendly and hospitable.' With that, the knight thanked the old man and rode on.

You will have noticed that there is a very powerful message in here, yet this is not a story directly about strategy. However, in reading it you may have made connections between the story and how you communicate your strategy, work with your teams or perhaps about other aspects of the way some people approach life.

One of the reasons this works is that people have to interpret the story for themselves and make their own associations. Rather than just saying, 'We are like this,' the metaphor allows you to make the connections yourself. You will often make the connection more deeply and extensively than with a direct message. For this reason, metaphors are very powerful.

113

I could have simply said, 'If you expect success or failure, you will be right.' I could have said, 'If you go through life expecting to meet gloomy people, you will find plenty of them.' You can see how the story, whilst being less direct, allows you to make these associations and many more, for yourself. Without the story it would not have had the same effect. I would have been appealing directly to your conscious thought to make the connections.

Storytelling is far older than the written word. For thousands of years, stories were a way of passing history, folklore and social norms through cultures. You can find such stories in a whole variety of places. Some people make up their own metaphors. Some use powerful stories from other situations. You can tell the story of how you found things in this book. There are lots of stories within your organization and in others you may have worked for. The key is to choose ones that have the essence of the message you are planning to get across, so people can make the connections for themselves.

Questions

Think of metaphors that are used in your organization: stories that are used indirectly to get a message across.

Which metaphors have a powerful message for you?

What powerful messages do you want to get across?

What stories might exemplify, reinforce and embed your message? (If you don't know of any, you can always design your own.)

METAPHORS IN THE LANGUAGE OF AN ORGANIZATION

Some organizations have their own language; in addition to their own jargon, you may notice another aspect of their language.

> *The organization was awash with metaphor. No matter where you went, there was a constant flow of language that was recycled again and again. The strategy was piped out to people, so they could tap into thinking. The management would be flushed with success. People would clean up their act. Careers would be in the fast stream.*

What sort of organization was this? Yes, as you have probably realized, it was a water and sewerage company. The clues were, of course, in the language. This is not unique. I have heard analogous patterns in organizations as diverse as finance, IT, research, retail, manufacturing and the nuclear industry.

These are a form of metaphor. They are ways of communicating ideas. People have aligned their language to that of the organization and what it does. For a career to be in the fast stream, there must also be a slow stream. The stream might also be blocked, or have run dry.

When you are presenting, be aware of what your language represents. Don't over do it, but be aware when you hear it and when it is used! You may find it used in some parts of the organization more than others; some departments will use it, whilst others may not. It may also depend upon the length of service of the person and whether they have been in that industry or company a long time.

This is different from the jargon of an organization or an industry, which you also need to be aware of. Internally, you will be expected to use and understand it. Externally, you might be expected not to use it, but to explain things in lay terms. In both cases, the key is consciousness. Are you using jargon? If you have just come from the power and electricity industry as a bright spark that used to light up the place, you may have to dampen down, or clean up, your style in a water company.

Questions

What language is common in your industry or organization?

Which parts of your organization use them the most? Is it peculiar to that part?

Do you want to play on this language or ignore it?

USING QUOTES

Many years ago a person said to me, 'A well chosen quote is worth a thousand pictures.' I didn't believe him until I tried using them. Now I realize how powerful they are and how right he was.

You may have already realized that I just made that quote up. It is the only quote in the book I have made up. Well chosen quotes are powerful ways of communicating a message.

Ways of using quotes

Here are eight ways of using quotes:

1. 'I just say, "STOP!" I ask myself, how can we continue like this any longer?'

    • Inviting others to share the quotation: by quoting yourself you are inviting people to say it to themselves.

2. 'I'm not going to say, "You need to follow up this book by using me as a consultant" because that would be too overt.'

- Saying what you are not going to say: however, have you noticed that I did in fact say it? People actually listen to the thing you said you are *not* going to say.

3. 'Some people might say they disagree, or "you are wrong", but I know that they have misunderstood my intentions.'

- By quoting 'some people', you are not actually saying this, or saying who did say it. You are simply saying, '*Some* people might say…'. Therefore, when you contradict it or reinforce it, you are not criticizing them directly.

4. 'I was chatting with a chief executive of a bank, and he told me how good these techniques were for communicating strategy…'

- Quoting an influential individual: here, you are not saying something directly. It is coming from someone else.

5. 'I said to myself, "This book has some really great ideas I can use."'

- By quoting yourself, you are being far less intrusive or direct, than simply saying, 'This book has some really powerful ideas you can use,' yet it has the same effect.

6. 'I sometimes ask myself, "Will this work?", but I know that I will only find out if I actually try it.'

- This asks a question and answerers it yourself, to anticipate or deflect the question in the first place.

7. 'I don't know if you are practising these out loud?'

- This has an embedded command within the sentence: 'Practise these out loud'. Embedded commands are all over the place and, now you have heard of them, you will start to notice them more and more, won't you?

8. 'Churchill said, "We shall fight them on the beaches".'

- Using a famous person's quotation to add emphasis to the statement – choose the quote and the person carefully.

As you listen to speech, especially that of people who are highly influential, you will start to notice that these patterns are actually very common.

Questions

Who do you know who uses quotes very effectively? How do they use them?

What message do you want to get across that might work well inside quotes?

Who could you quote?

Actively gather quotes from people. When I am doing reviews of projects with my clients, and I hear a great quote, I say, 'May I use that?' The client is normally delighted to be quoted.

Quotes are effective because they are less direct than actually telling someone something directly. If I said, 'This is simply the best book on communicating strategy,' you would think I was both biased and blowing my own trumpet. That is why books have quotes from people other than the author on the cover. Those people carry a weight that is independent and in many cases have their own authority.

Quotes are also a useful way to send an otherwise tricky messages to someone. You might say, 'I came across someone in my old organization who was leaking information to a competitor, and I said to them, "That is completely unacceptable! If you leak a single word of this to any of our competitors, you will be sacked!"' By pointing at the audience as you say it, you are not saying directly to anyone that they have communicated information to a competitor, but you are making it clear that the quote applies to them as much as it does to the person in the story.

Of course, there are times when you may want to say this message directly so it is completely unequivocal and unambiguous. If you are saying to a person or group that they have done wrong, do not use quotes, as it will dilute the message.

Sources of quotes

Where might these quotes come from? There are lots of people whom you could quote. Remember that choosing whom to quote will also have an effect. Have a think about:

- customers
- investors
- competitors
- staff
- business gurus
- yourself
- management team members
- the audience

I put customer quotes at the top of the list, as these are often the most powerful. When a customer says to me, 'That was simply the best training I have had for years,' or the managing director says, 'That was the most effective workshop I have ever being involved in,' I make a point of thanking them and writing it down immediately. I also ask whether they are happy to be quoted. This is both a matter of courtesy and good risk management. You will be breaching copyright laws if you publish a letter of thanks on your website without the author's permission. This seems extreme, so be sure that you have asked whether they are happy to be quoted in this way.

If you are working in a charity or another not-for-profit organization (such as local government or health) where you are serving a community, the members of that community are also great sources of quotes and anecdotes.

The Internet is a great source of quotes for various topics. Simply by typing 'quotes business' or 'quotes communication' or any other topic, into a search engine you can find whole sites devoted to quotes by famous people, ranging from philosophers to business people, politicians to actors.

Questions

What quotes do you already have that would be useful?

Who could you go to for quotes?

Who can collect quotes for you?

Who can you quote?

PACING AND LEADING PEOPLE

Have you noticed how comedians or performers will often start with 'Hello … Chicago/London/Dublin', or whatever city they are in?

Have you noticed how some presenters start with something like, 'Well, here we are on a bright sunny day in London and the previous speaker has given some great insights into presenting well. Now we are going to build upon that by looking specifically at communicating strategy…'?

Perhaps you can recall a time when you have been talking with someone and gradually you notice that someone else has joined the conversation. They seem to have effortlessly eased their way into the conversation.

Now contrast that with the situation where you are talking with someone and another person comes across and just tramples all over the conversation. You were connected with someone when, suddenly, someone has trampled on the connection. This happened to me recently at a networking event. I was chatting with someone I had not seen for a year, getting an update on how her business had been developing, when someone just walked up to us and said, 'Hi, I'm John.' We both just looked at him aghast. In this case, the person simply did not pace himself into the conversation; he just butted in.

The comedians, on the other hand, are building rapport with the audience by referring to their current and recent experience. In the case of the presenter referring to a previous presenter, they are making a link, apparently seamlessly, from the context of the previous presentation, to the content of their presentation. These people are 'pacing and leading'. They match or pace a person's current experience and then start to lead them towards where you want them to be. The comedian is pacing with their experience of the city. The presenter is pacing the experience of previous presenters and their environment. The effective networker is pacing the conversation, looking for clues, starting to nod and agree at the same point that the others are and perhaps easing themselves in when an opportunity presents itself.

A variation of this approach, often used by sales people and politicians, is the 'yes' pattern. This goes something like, 'Are you sitting comfortably?' 'Are you reading this book?' 'Are you finding things that will help you improve?' 'Are you willing to recommend this book to others as well?' Here, you are setting up a pattern of getting 'yes' answers. By moving from a simple question, where the answer is 'yes', to a slightly deeper question and another still so you have a sequence of 'yes' answers. When you ask the final question, the person is already in a 'yes' frame of mind. If you were to step right in with, 'Would you like to buy some double glazing?', you can guess what the answer would be.

This process establishes rapport with the group or team to whom you are presenting the strategy. Assess where they are at the moment and their recent and current experiences. This provides a base to pace their thinking and frame of mind, to acknowledge them and their thinking, so you can start to lead them to where you want them to go.

Questions

What is the recent experience of the groups you are dealing with?

What is the energy level of the groups you are dealing with?

How could you acknowledge these and match them?

Do you want to match them?

Leading, then pacing

You don't have to pace and lead. You could lead, and then pace. Leading and pacing takes a different approach.

Think of high-energy presenters, or people who burst onto the stage, or simply walk into a room and the whole energy level changes. Their energy changes the atmosphere of the whole room. Have you ever been to a concert or presentation where, suddenly, they start punching high-energy rock music into the auditorium to set the tone for the presentations or sessions that follow?

These events are designed to lead and then get people to follow. High-energy presenters get people engaged, create a sense of empowerment and shared enthusiasm. This approach can work very well. It is an approach that requires a certain amount or charisma and energy. It also requires an audience with whom you are willing to take a risk.

To lead and pace requires a different approach to pacing and leading. It involves:

- having a positive state with high energy;

- being clear about where you want to go;

- communicating things as you see them;

- getting the reaction;

- opening up to accept where people want to go;

- starting by pacing them, and leading them from there.

The high-energy approach is about deliberately breaking rapport to get things moving. You will notice that there is still, within this process, a pacing stage. It happens much later in the process. If they simply pumped up the energy and kept pumping it up, they would be likely to lose people. You will notice changes of energy, moments when the presenter reconnects with the audience to pick them up and take them along to the next energy rush. Quite often these will be picked up through metaphor and stories, as we have discussed previously. You still need a clear understanding of people's current state and recent experiences. You still need to establish rapport, but you are setting the standard and being clear about where you want to go.

Questions

What is the recent experience of the groups you are dealing with?

What is the energy level of the groups you are dealing with?

What is your energy level?

Is there enough implicit pacing that you could start leading them, and pace them afterwards?

You will have realized that pacing and leading, or leading and pacing, are both similar to the 'away from' and 'towards' mentality that we explored earlier. You may need to 'pace, then lead' if someone is in an 'away from' mentality. Alternatively, if they are already in a 'towards' mind-set, then it is easier to 'lead, then pace'. Those who have already paid their money to go and see a motivational speaker have already self-selected themselves and made a positive commitment to change, and so are already in a 'towards' mind-set.

WINNING THEIR HEARTS AND MINDS

We have already talked about a number of ways in which you can make the story of the strategy more compelling. You have already seen how you can develop a rich picture of the strategy and get a feel for how to pace and to lead people along the journey. You may have noticed that, in telling the story of how to communicate your strategy, we are explicitly giving you a taste of what it is like to communicate the strategy effectively.

Another aspect of making the story compelling is using language that ensures you engage all the people in the audience. Have you ever noticed how some people just don't seem to understand what you mean? Have you ever noticed how, with some people, they just don't *see* what you mean? Perhaps others don't have a *feel* for what you are getting at? Some may not like the *sound* of what you are saying. This is because individuals have a variety of styles of thinking and language that they tend to prefer. Some people prefer to 'see' things. They use a lot of visual metaphors in their language. You will hear some people use a lot of auditory language. You may like the 'sound' of that. Some like to get the 'feel' of problems and rely on gut instinct. Others may have a 'taste' for things, or are good at 'sniffing out' a problem. Of course, it is always useful to have the facts, figures and evidence and some people will have a preference for these.[1]

These patterns of language encompassing the visual, auditory and kinaesthetic occur because of the various styles of thinking we prefer and the senses we tend to use most, internally, to store and refer to external events. You will notice this when listening to how people recall an event. Some will remember what they saw, others how it felt, or sounded and others will remember the detail. When communicating with a group or people or a large audience, you need to use all these different styles to ensure you connect with all the different individuals.

People do not just belong to just one category. This is really important. We all have all of the senses. It is just that some senses are more strongly developed in particular people. Some people have a preference to use a certain type of sense language before others. It is not a case that you might be entirely visual or kinaesthetic; it is simply that you are stronger in or prefer visual to the other senses.

There is no right or wrong here. It is not better to have a kinaesthetic or visual preference. Obviously, if you are a singer, it is helpful to have a well developed auditory sense, but singers will also have a feeling for the music and may imagine pitching their notes at various places around them.

---

1   The representation systems described here are generally referred to as a part of Neuro-Linguistic Programming (NLP). However, they have been recognized long before NLP.

As you work through this section, you will start to notice your preferred styles, the preferred styles of those with whom you work, and those of other presenters. Ensure that you balance the styles and representation systems you use in presentations so that you include and touch all the members of the audience, in their own way, so they *see*, *feel* and *hear* the message.

Keeping an eye out

When the language is very visual you will see clearly what the differences are. People with a visual preference will tend to show you something, draw diagrams or want to be convinced by seeing how something works. They will like the look of things, and want to see things to be convinced.

You will notice that visual people tend to think and talk faster than the other groups. This is because they construct their pictures very quickly. They will tend to look up and often be constructing, or remembering, pictures in front of them or slightly above them. When they do this they are not ignoring you, they are playing what you have said in their existing pictures, or recalling things that will add to the conversation. They may also change their minds more easily, as the pictures they have created get refined and updated.

You may have had a teacher at school who would ask a question and then say to a pupil, 'The answer is not on the ceiling.' Well, they were wrong, because for that child, the answer was on the ceiling (or at least upwards and in front of them). That is where they stored it. By forcing the child not to look up, they were actually preventing them from accessing the answer. Sad, isn't it?

So keep an eye out for how people use imagery when you see them speak. Table 7.1 lists some common imagery language.

To engage these people you need to show them things. They will like pictures, drawings, videos, brochures, photographs, diagrams and graphs. You will need to paint pictures with your words.

Questions

How much do you use this language and representational system?

Who do you know who is strongly visual?

What do you notice about how they speak, think and work?

Liking the sound of

When you hear language full of auditory clues, it will sound like there are a lot of words that describe what you might hear; auditory listeners will be tuned into the tone of voice and effective communication will need to sound good. They may want to hear things in order to be convinced.

Table 7.1   Imagery language

view	lacklustre	reflect	dark
vision	shine	dim	unclear
sparkle	vivid	crystal clear	dull
colourful	scene	blue sky	keep an eye on
perspective	mirror	brighten	whole picture
watch	snap shot	opaque	highlights
show	brilliant	obscure	see

You may notice that strongly auditory people tend to lean their head to one side to hear what is being said and will pay more attention to voice tonality. They are more likely to vary their pitch more when speaking and they will want you to be on their wavelength.

Listen out for examples of auditory language when people are talking. Table 7.2 provides some examples.

To engage these people, you need to ensure they like the sound of what you are doing, can speak out and that you use auditory language in your communication.

Questions

How much do you use this language and representational system?

Who do you know who is strongly auditory?

What do you notice about how they speak, think and work?

Having a feeling for

When the language is more about feelings you are likely to be dealing with a kinaesthetic preference. These people will like the feel of things, to be hands on and grasp the situation. They will put their feelers out, get a grasp on things and touch the people, or expect to be touched, in a way that makes a difference.

Table 7.2   Auditory language

hear	tune in	rumour	articulate
listen	accent	mumble	amplify
ring to it	tone	resound	note
sounds like	buzz	remark	proclaim
quiet	echo	chord	utter
tell	loud	compose	vocal
be all ears	wavelength	discuss	shouts
speak	music to my ears	announce	silence

One characteristic of kinaesthetic people is that they will often pause and take a breath before answering a question. They are actually checking in with their body (the primary place where they store their kinaesthetic feelings) before answering you. They will then give you the answer that feels right. Having absorbed the question into their body, they now own it more, they have internalized the answer in a way that the visual person will not necessarily have done. Thus a kinaesthetic may take more convincing to change, as they will want to re-internalize their new set of feelings. However, having done so, they may be more committed to the answer than, say, a dominantly visual person.

One particular team of managers happened to be all dominantly kinaesthetic. They felt they were on the right track, but also felt stuck. As a dominantly visual person, I was asked to work with them to help them test their model and see some alternatives. In effect I was to break into their existing pattern of thinking.

After two hours they had a new model, but declared they had to stop. They decided the pain and anguish was too much. They needed to go to the pub for a couple of hours and let what we had done sink in. Their new sense of what they now had was quite different from their old one and felt uncomfortable initially. Once they had had a chance to mull things over, they came back that afternoon, strongly owning the new model as theirs.

To get a feel for kinaesthetic language, notice how they use words such as those in Table 7.3.

Table 7.3   Kinaesthetic language

feel	touch	sense	lukewarm
sharp	get hold of	solid	shallow
impact	get to grips with	heavy	shock
itchy	get a feel for	light	tickle
rough	gritty	robust	handle
smooth	uptight	pain	gentle
sensitive	knotted stomach	love	cold
bumpy	feelers	pleasure	warm

To engage a kinaesthetic, give them a chance to touch, get a feel for and sense what is going on. You may also need to give them time to internalize it.

Questions

How much do you use this language and representational system?

Who do you know who is strongly kinaesthetic?

What do you notice about how they speak, think and work?

Getting a taste for

You may also come across people whose language includes words like bitter, sour, sweet and tasty. They won't like the smell of something. These people are using gustatory (taste) and olfactory (smell) language.

To get a taste of what we are talking about, look at the words in Table 7.4.

Notice that some words can come from different representational systems. Light can be both visual (bright) and kinaesthetic (not heavy). Soft could be quiet or gentle. Clear could be transparent or as clear as a bell.

Table 7.4   Gustatory and Olfactory language

smell	bitter	the sweet smell of	salivate
sniff	sour	bland	imbibe
bad taste	sweet	fishy	whet your
whiff of a	bad odour	fragrant	appetite
problem	smells iffy	tasty	hunger for
after taste	smells wrong	rotten	starve
lick			sip success

Questions

How much do you use this language and representational system?

Who do you know who is strongly gustatory or olfactory?

What do you notice about how they speak, think and work?

Logic and intuition

So far we have used categorizations of language and thinking patterns from Neuro-Linguistic Programming (NLP). However, there is another category that is to do with being convinced by logic. These people are convinced by rational argument, seeing the facts, having the numbers, analyzing the statistics and examining the evidence.

These people will tend to use a non-sensory language, one that is more logical or analytical. They want to explore the information, understand the theory, test the implications and know what is going on. Again, this is not a trait that exists on its own. You will come across engineers or accountants who like the evidence, but have a feel for the implications, or see the consequences, and like the sound of the numbers.

To get an understanding of the logic of this you will have evidence of words such as those in Table 7.5.

Table 7.5   Analytical language

theory	prove	systematic	interpretation
numbers	demonstrate	process	concept
facts	experience	source of	usual
knowledge	application	specific	idea
information	benefit	procedure	virtual
evidence	value	calculation	programme

To engage such people make sure you provide the facts and evidence to support your arguments.

Questions

How much do you rely on logic and fact? How much on intuition?

Who do you know who is strongly 'fact based'? Who do you know who relies on intuition?

What do you notice about how they speak, think and behave?

Internal and external frames of reference

Individuals, and whole organizations, operate a frame of reference by which they judge things. Some people carry a very strong internal frame of reference. No matter how well you tell them they are doing, whether it is good or bad, they will apply their own internal judgement set.

Likewise, I have met really strong people who still need to have someone else say that they are doing a good job. Despite all their strong attributes, they need external validation.

The same applies to organizations. I have met organizations that are obsessed by their ranking in an industry and by the need to have everything benchmarked against peers or 'world-class' organizations. Put a benchmark in front of them and they are happy, no matter how inappropriate the comparison group or organization is. They ask questions about the right amount to spend on IT, compliance, service, as if copying everyone else is always the answer. They may often, openly, set out to win industry awards.

In public sector bodies such as health, the police and local government, this comparison approach is used a lot. Whole public sector bodies, such as the Audit Commission in the UK, exist substantially to provide these comparisons.

In contrast, many organizations would not dream of benchmarking themselves (unless it helped make the case for how good they were to those who need it). These organizations have an inner confidence that how they do it is the best way. They might believe that by benchmarking, all they are doing is copying 'common practice' rather than getting 'best practice'.[2]

It is useful to show comparative information to those who need external validation as a convincer. This is particularly useful when you are making the case for change and demonstrating how far behind you may have become. It can also be useful to explain what good practice should look like and what level of performance is possible.

Balance this with an emphasis on pride and self-confidence. By emphasizing how these organizations feel in themselves, and what pride they can have, you are appealing to an internal frame of reference. Sometimes you are giving them permission to be proud of themselves and what they have achieved, as opposed to always thinking of themselves as second best.

Looking at things from the customer's perspective does provide such a frame of reference. Your people may think you provide an excellent service, yet they need to be awakened by hearing and seeing what the customers actually think of the service. The external frame of reference of real customers saying what they think, feel and have incurred as consequential costs, can have a powerful effect. Of course, this also provides a powerful source of quotations.

Questions

How does your organization judge itself today?

How do the groups judge themselves today:

- *against an external frame of reference?*
- *against internal standards?*

What external information and evidence do you have that will help convince people of where they are and what needs changing?

What do you have that will appeal to people's sense of pride in the job and their internal reference points?

Why, what, how and what if?

The way people think about things and represent them internally in their language representation systems does affect how they prefer to experience and be convinced of things. However, there are other learning styles that can be incorporated into your presentations.

---

2   There is 'common practice', 'good practice' and 'best practice'. Unfortunately my experience is that much of what is passed off as best practice is merely common (and often not even good). Some people and organizations even 'hype this up' by saying what they do is 'world class'. Rarely do you hear them say (far more honestly) that this is European class or the best in the nation.

In the 1970s, Bernice McCarthy,[3] a teacher, noticed that various children tended to ask specific, but different questions in class. Some would ask, 'Why?': why are we doing this? and why does this happen? Others would ask 'How?': how do these things work and how do I do this? Another group would tend to ask for facts and information and wanted to know 'What?': what is going on? Where do they come from? What does that mean? There were also some children who wanted to understand the implications of things and the consequences: if this happened, then what would happen next? If I learn this, what can I use it for? What will happen if I do this? What happens if I don't do this?

McCarthy noticed that most education is focused on the 'what' and provides facts and information. Far less addresses the 'why', 'how' and 'what if' questions. This recognition led to an approach that is called the 4MAT system (Table 7.6). Her solution was to ensure that she addressed all four learning styles in every explanation.

So, in planning how to communicate strategy, ensure you address the four styles: why you are communicating, what information you will provide and what benefits they will get, how people will learn and experience the session and how it can be applied today, and what they can do with it and the consequences of applying it or failing to apply it.

Anchoring experiences

People often associate emotional states with particular experiences, messages or events. Some places, music and people remind you of things. If you had a bad experience at the last sales conference, then going to the same place with the same speakers may not go down well. If the organization has made people redundant by sending a letter home, then guess what you will think when the next company letter comes through the door. I once interviewed a manager who started by saying that the only previous time he had being interviewed by a consultant, he had ended up being made redundant. This is called 'anchoring': a set of emotions is associated with a place, person, or perhaps

Table 7.6   The 4MAT System

Question	Preferred approach	Learning style	%
Why?	Reasons and explanations	Discussion	35%
What?	Data and information	Teaching	22%
How?	Hands-on experience	Coaching	18%
What if?	Group discussions and self exploration	Self-discovery	25%

---

3   McCarthy, B., in James, T. and Shepherd, D. (2001), *Presenting Magically* (Carmarthen, Wales: Crown House Publishing), pp. 177–181.

that music. The same thing will be true in your organization. Certain things, places and messages will be associated with certain emotions. Organizations may change the environment and move offices to break the association, to provide a different context and make a fresh start.

Sometimes the anchoring process is quite subtle. I watched a facilitator carefully isolate the frustrating issues in a workshop, write them up on a flip chart, and then attach the flip chart to inside of the door. Despite all the good work during the day, at the end, they reverted back to their original thinking. What had he done? He had anchored the issues and problems on to the flipchart on the door. He kept referring to them and so, when they left, they walked straight back through them, taking the issues with them. If he had associated them with a far corner that they had walked away from, it would not have happened. In contrast, if you put the summary of actions on the door, people are likely to associate with them as they leave.

This same approach is used by many professionals. Comedians use anchoring to train the audience when to laugh at a particular point on the stage or gesture they make. Sports people and athletes use anchoring to get ready for a golf swing, or a race. Good presenters may use it to indicate a mood, anchor a symbolic future at a point on the stage, or stand at a particular point on the stage whenever they speak as if they were a supplier or customer.

Look out for how people who do this. Be aware of how you anchor emotions and situations, intentionally or otherwise.

ENCOURAGING AND DISCOURAGING FEEDBACK

When you explain and tell the story of your strategy, you should be looking for three pieces of feedback:

1.   people seeking to understand what is being said;

2.   people understanding what the change will mean to them;

3.   people seeking to make a contribution.

Feedback is about listening and learning. Unfortunately, there are ways in which we (unintentionally) discourage feedback and constructive comments. We fail to learn from our communication. It is really easy to stifle debate, kill feedback and discourage people from contributing. Have you ever been shut up in a meeting? Have you ever met someone who says that they tried asking, but gave up? Have you ever had a presenter who killed the question or effectively shot the questioner? The skill of killing dissenters and discouraging input is more common than it should be. The techniques are used too regularly. The following examples show what some do to kill feedback and how to avoid them.

Don't ask for it, or allow it

One of the simplest ways of discouraging feedback is simply not to ask for it, or to remove the opportunity for it: 'That is the session over: now back to work!' By not even giving the opportunity for questions, you are preventing feedback. To avoid this, encourage openness by asking questions. Make sure that you leave adequate time for questions and that you ask for them. Be clear at the start of the session whether you want questions at the end, or as you go along.

If you use one-way channels you will also limit feedback. Give long presentations to a large number of people without questions. Use newsletters, videos and other channels that tell, but do not communicate. Go through the channels you have selected previously and ensure that you are both communicating and listening. There are times when you want to get the message out. There are times when you want to hear the feedback and be refining the message and the story or even the strategy. Appendix A provides a review of the most popular channels and includes assessments of their potential for feedback.

Be sarcastic

Sarcasm is the lowest form of wit. A few years ago the expression, 'Thank you for that,' was very popular as a killing response to unwelcome questions or comments. It was best delivered in a somewhat sarcastic tone and sent a clear message that the contribution was unwelcome. To make sure you don't do this, acknowledge questions graciously. Repeat the question, so that others can also hear it, in a grateful manner, such as, 'Susan has asked ...'. You will avoid sarcasm if your attitude to the audience is positive and open.

Attack the questioner

Responses like, 'That's a very unhelpful question,' or 'You must be mad asking that,' are the equivalent of firing a missile at the questioner. What you are doing is attacking the person rather that the question. People will notice. To avoid this, always respect the questioner and ensure that you address the question rather than the questioner. Respect the questioner, address the question.

Dismiss the question or questioner

Answering, 'I have already answered that,' when you have not, effectively ignores the questioner and question. You haven't even given them the chance to ask the question. In this case the person is not attacking the questioner, but disparaging the question itself. Even if you have already answered it, answer it again. Maybe you didn't get the message across. Maybe they missed it. Maybe you forgot to say it. Maybe you were not clear. Acknowledge the question, don't dismiss the question.

Pass it off for later

Sometimes questions are brushed aside, 'We are not going to answer that now.' This is a useful approach when you are saying that the question is off the agenda. However, if you do this a lot, especially to valid questions, you will undermine the message and your credibility. Ultimately questions will become permanently off the agenda and you will have discouraged feedback and questions. To avoid this, *visibly* park the question. Acknowledge the question, say why you are parking it, ensure that the question is noted and make it clear that you will return to it, at a different time and place. Make sure you do return to it.

Waffle

If you do not know the answer, do not waffle. Admit that you do not know the answer, say what you will do to find out and get back to the person who asked it. Don't waffle.

Don't feel under pressure to say something quickly. Take the time to reflect on an answer if you need to. You will be surprised how long you can hold a silence for, whilst you think of the most appropriate answer. Listeners respect this, because it seems a more considered answer than simply shooting from the hip. If you do need time to think about the question, or you are unsure, you can always repeat the question back, to check that you heard it correctly. Remember to answer the question that was asked, rather than the one you thought you heard. You can also ask the questioner to clarify what they meant by expanding on the question. The clarification often makes the question easier to address.

The politician's answer

People who are regularly interviewed by the media ensure that they have a clear message or agenda they want to get across. Being clear about this enables them to answer questions in the way the want to. You will recognize the pattern. In response to the question, 'Why has your department failed to deliver any improvements over the last five years?', they might reply, 'You know some people may say that the department is failing, but when you look at the figures, you can see that we have had a 20 per cent increase in the take up of this benefit and that more and more people are coming out of poverty. Moreover we are serving more people as the government provides more support for the under privileged.' The answer would be the same for any question. The question is acknowledged, denied and then the statement that they want to make is made. This is one of the very first lessons of media training. Have a clear message and link from the question actually asked to the statement that you want to say.[4]

---

4   For more examples like this see, Stevens, A. (2005), *The Pocket Media Coach* (Oxford: Howtobooks). Alternatively listen to some of his presentations, available from his website www. mediacoach.co.uk.

If you do this too often, too blatantly, or make tenuous links, you will gain a reputation for not answering the question. However, with practice, you will be able to make a smooth transition from the awkward question to the message you want to get across. The key is knowing the clear message you wish to communicate.

Answering dissenters

There are times when it will be necessary to handle a dissenter.

> *When presenting a change of working arrangements to a factory workforce, there were one or two people who were particularly vocal. The management had already assessed seven options, discussed them with a sub-set of worker representatives and narrowed them down, with their help, to just two options. The overall situation was being explained and the two options were now being presented to the workforce, so they could vote on them. One particular person was quite vocal. He suggested that there should be more alternatives and that he wanted more involvement.*
>
> *The managing director gave the workforce representatives a chance to explain what had gone on to get them to here, but the person was still vocal. In the end the managing director simply said, 'Look, you elected these workforce representatives to have these discussions on your behalf. That is their role. We used them and now we are talking to you. If we had come to the table with all of you with all seven options we would have still being debating this in 9 months time. Do you have a constructive alternative? If so, tell me. If not, let's get on debating the two that your representatives have chosen and get on with the vote.'*
>
> *After the meeting, the dissenting individual came up to the managing director. He admitted he had no alternatives and just felt that they ought to have been talked to earlier. The managing director restated the position and explained that the role of their representatives also needed to include confidentiality. Otherwise, what was the point of having them and trusting them? The dissenter agreed.*

Sometimes you will have to state your position clearly. Be clear about the principles you are working from and the rules of the game that you have established. In this case, a workforce representatives existed precisely for these discussions.

How can I contribute?

In gathering feedback you will get people asking how they can contribute to the strategy. The normal mechanisms will be through their line managers, but there are other ways to do this.

Take over a conference room and dedicate it to the project. Leave it open for 24 hours and encourage people to come into it. Publish all the information on the walls, staff it full time, and invite people to come in and discuss it.

Create discussion opportunities and ask for their support and contribution. Open up a discussion forum, or blog, on the organization's intranet. Encourage questions and responses.

Provide time and opportunities in the briefing sessions. Ensure people can access pictures or documents from the strategy and review them. By providing sticky notes, people can attach their comments to the strategy.

Following the directors' summaries of the strategy, we encouraged questions and then gave everyone sticky notes. The strategy maps had been printed on A0 posters and attached to the walls. We said, go up to them and put as many sticky notes as you like on them. We are looking particularly for:

- *comments and support;*

- *disagreements;*

- *where you can help.*

This feedback was then written up and circulated around the team. The functional directors were responsible for getting back to the staff who had commented on their strategy (and left their name as well), whether they were in their department or not.

Questions

How are you going to encourage people to think about where they can contribute?

How will you gather people's contributions?

What channels and events are you using to ensure this happens?

A final word on feedback

This is not an exhaustive list. To get better at recognizing these styles, and others, listen to political interviews on the radio or television. Notice your reaction to the first few words of the response to a question and what they actually said. Is the question being answered or is it being avoided?

There is no excuse for these inappropriate techniques being used. There are plenty of ways to handle an awkward question using the quotes we talked about earlier. For instance, 'Many have asked that, but they have come to realize that there is a better way,' or, 'We had that question from a customer as well, so we explained ...' It comes down to the attitude and confidence of the presenter. Techniques for killing feedback seem most common where people feel defensive. When presenters are open and congruent, the questions are encouraged and answered.

I have seen people who have only used these techniques a couple of times in the wrong circumstances, only to completely discouraged input and questions almost permanently. It only takes a couple of situations in which questions are killed or the questioner is attacked, and you will annoy and alienate the audience, kill input and discourage further questioning.

It can become institutionalized. I have come across organizations that have systematically trained their staff *not* to be constructive and *not* to contribute. They have done it, persistently, over long period, until they are quite used to it and don't even realize that it has happened. Then they wonder why they don't get much out of their people.

Questions

Does your organization have a culture that constrains feedback?

Have you trained your staff so they are aware of these pitfalls and how to avoid them?

What can you do to encourage feedback?

There is an expression, 'The meaning of the feedback is the response it gets.' When you say (or write) something and get a response, the response may not be what you expect. You have asked a question, from your perspective. The other person has heard the question and responded, not from your perspective, but from theirs.

The response you get reflects their interpretation of the question. It may not be what you expected, but it does provide you with an insight into how they see and interpret the world. You are getting the meaning that they attach to your statement. So the meaning, to them, of what you said, will come back to you as feedback that you can use to understand that person's perspective better. Be open to these messages. They may not be what you expected as an answer. They will give you a great insight into what others are actually thinking and what is important for them.

There is a similar saying, 'There is no failure, only feedback.' In other words, you didn't fail to communicate; you simply got some feedback that you were not expecting. If a comedian tells a joke that dies, they can think of it as a failure and give up telling jokes. If they think of it as feedback about that joke, told that way, with that audience, then they can change some aspects, so that next time they tell it differently. This treats the feedback as useful information, rather than judging it (or yourself) as successful or failing. Then you have used the feedback.

Questions

Think of a time when you have asked a question and not received the response you expected. What was it about the other person's perspective that was different from yours and would explain their response?

What feedback are you getting about your strategy that was unexpected? What does it mean?

CONCLUSION

In engaging people's hearts and minds, we have described a variety of different ways in which people think, represent things, use language and learn. The representational systems (visual, auditory, kinaesthetic, olfactory and gustatory) from NLP, suggest ensuring that you give people a feel for things as well as talking to and showing them. Using facts, as well as feelings, plays an important role to ensure you address the needs of those who want evidence as well those who rely on their intuition.

Some people will prefer to see how they compare against others and be told how they are doing by others, whilst some will prefer their own internal standards by which they wish to meet and judge themselves. Some want to know what they will learn; others how they can use it; some prefer why it is important, or even, what will happen if we don't do it.

Fortunately, we are not all alike. Whilst this may seem a bewildering list of things to consider in a presentation, and in communicating the strategy, it emphasizes an important point. Others will think in different ways and patterns to you. Be aware of this and ensure that you address both their, and your, preferred patterns. Then you are more likely to engage the people and get across your message. Failure to do this might only engage a small fraction of the audience at most.

You can bring these techniques and ways of talking and expressing yourself into your communication and into your stories and metaphors. By combining the most appropriate, compelling and insightful stories and metaphors, with a compelling and engaging style of speech, you are more likely to engage more people, and to get your message across, so more get it.

To make it easy for you, use this simple checklist:

- Have I got stories that reinforce the messages I am trying to get across?

- Have I got metaphors that help communicate the message?

- Have I got quotes I can build into my presentations that will widen the appeal and improve the message?

- Have I engaged people by covering the four aspects of the 4MAT system in my introduction?

- Am I using words from the main representational systems: seeing, feeling, hearing and giving people a taste of things?

- Am I creating internal and external points of reference? Am I providing facts to back this up?

- Am I combining these together in a natural manner?

- Am I allowing and encouraging feedback on the story?

As has been emphasized all the way through, the art of telling the story of the strategy also relies on the integrity of the storyteller: does your audience believe you? Are they aligned behind your strategy?

Finally, remember we have two ears and one mouth, and we should use them in that proportion, even when we are communicating our strategy.

8 The Aligned Management Team

Have you ever seen presenters whose language and words appear inconsistent with their body language? Something does not feel right. As you listen, you just get that feeling that they do not mean what they say. Quite often you are not even sure why you know this: you just do. The presenter does not look as if they are talking with integrity or belief in what they are saying. They look unaligned. It simply leaks out when this happens.

The same can be true of an organization. An organization is a living entity. The overall corporate message is the sum of all the individual messages it sends out. Listeners will quickly notice a lack of integrity or consistency amongst these messages. This will undermine the message about your strategy and could lead to your strategy not succeeding.

This chapter, and the subsequent one, explore how this can happen, how you will recognize it, its consequences and what you can do about it. The next chapter covers inconsistency caused by the organization's policies, processes and activities. This chapter covers one of the most obvious signs of a misaligned organization: when the management team each give out different messages, and what might cause that to happen.

IDEAL SITUATION

You should be in a situation where the management team are telling the same story of the strategy. What should happen?

The communication from the chief executive should be consistent with and use the same material as all the other directors. All the next level and middle managers are given the same briefings and hearing the same story. All are equipped to tell a consistent story to their staff and to answer their questions appropriately. Their briefings, whether to small groups or larger assemblies, should tell a consistent message. If some groups of people are affected differently from others, there must be specific messages for those people. These messages about the strategy should be consistent no matter where they come from; the Internet, company newspaper, team briefings, and announcements to the press or outside world.

Who should lead the communication of the strategy? This should be the chief executive, the chief executive, or the chief executive. Take your pick.

Consistency of message usually comes from thorough preparation and planning; just the sort of preparation and planning you have been developing and thinking about as you have read this book. Well rehearsed presentations, carefully crafted slides, well edited briefings and papers all form a part of this message.

If questions can't be answered immediately, they should be fed back through the system so that they are addressed and that others are also aware of the additional answers that are available. All this builds to a consistent message communicated well.

If there are examples of poor communication, where the message has not got through or the audience has been left in a state of uncertainty or ambiguity, then these should be addressed.

INCONSISTENT MESSAGES

The most obvious sign of a misaligned organization occurs when different members of the management team give out different messages. If you are describing quite different strategies, then you have no choice but to return to square one and resolve the issue in the boardroom. More likely, senior managers may be describing a different understanding of the same strategy. They agree on and state the same broad objectives, components, themes and aims but differ in the detail, interpretation and action. In these cases you have additional work to do, depending upon the cause. This confusion can be caused by a number of things.

It may be that the strategy has come from one main person, and hasn't been fully explained and integrated by the other members of the management team. My experience of meeting senior executives who have developed the strategy, but then say, 'They don't get it' has been the origin of this book.

Misunderstandings often arise when the patterns of thinking and language have been at cross purposes. It may also happen if debate has been unintentionally stifled in any meetings: those present may not have had a chance to test their understanding of what the strategy all means. They may be using the same words, but these words represent different ideas for the various people. It may have been assumed that they already understand the strategy. The discussions may have been cut short and the time for discussion limited, so others have not had a chance to assimilate all the information.

A director was concerned that his colleagues seemed inconsistent when describing the strategy of channels to market. It was only when we explored the channels in detail that he realized that there were several subtly different routes to market. He understood why he had been confused. They had been talking about different channels at different times. Moreover, the confused director had felt uncomfortable bringing up his confusion. Meanwhile, the other directors discussing the channels were so busy resolving their understanding amongst themselves, that they had not realized others in the room were still confused.

It is an important role of the leader of the team, usually the chief executive, to ensure that everyone understands the same thing. They need to look around the room and ensure that understanding is shared; to make time for discussion and debate and to check that others also understand. If there is not time within the meeting, they should make sure that a marker is put down to resolve the understanding outside the meeting. Pride should not lead to ignorance. An apparently stupid question can reveal a misconception that others share as well.

SILO AND FUNCTIONAL FOCUS

One reason for a lack of debate can be the different roles occupied by members of the management team. They may operate as a collection of departmental managers, or functional specialists, rather than as a general management team.

I have seen this behaviour demonstrated by various other functional directors, such as finance, human resources and sales. The specialist director concentrates on their own department, rather than being a general manager with a specific portfolio. In some cases these managers had come up a narrow career path and found it difficult to move into a more general management role. In other cases, they were pigeonholed by the other directors. Many were never given the training and opportunity to take on a wider role. When a new board member joins the team, others can be unintentionally sidelined or excluded in discussions.

This functional, or silo, thinking in the boardroom can be a symptom of solo operations in the organization as a whole, where departments fail to communicate with one another.

It is the responsibility of all the members of the team, but especially the chief executive, to ensure team members operate effectively. It is part of their career development responsibility to develop their team so that functional managers are able to think more corporately strategically, as well as bringing a functional specialism to the table.

INCONSISTENCY BETWEEN WORDS AND ACTIONS

A subtle version of misalignment within the message of the strategy occurs when what is said is different from what is done. This is the difference between what is espoused, and the actions and behaviours that people see.[1]

Sometimes this is quite blatant. A person may say they will do something, and then do something else, or fail to do it at all. They may give verbal support to an initiative, but behind the scenes they are undermining things to undermine the initiative. This sort of duplicitous behaviour is called 'malicious compliance'.

140

A more subtle example is where the message itself is mixed. Imagine a manager telling one of their staff that they want them to learn, take more responsibility and be self-sufficient. The conversation might go, 'I want to delegate responsibility to you, so you learn and develop. I want less involvement and for you to stand on your own two feet. You are responsible for this now and accountable for it. Of course, if you need anything, just come and ask and I will sort it out.'

Notice how the last sentence completely undermines the previous message. It seems a good intention, but by saying they will sort things out, they undermine all the self-determination. The final sentence may not be articulated but the actions of the manager working in the background have the same undermining effect. Whilst they have good intentions, and want to help the employee, their inability to let go undermines the message they intend to give.

BREAKING RANKS

It is possible that someone decides to break ranks and send a different message out. They might disagree with the strategy. They might feel threatened. They might have wanted the chief executive's job and missed out. They might be planning to leave.

Whatever the reason, this is a dangerous situation that needs putting right very quickly. You may give them a chance to 'get on the bus' and put things right. You will probably prefer to put things right behind closed doors in the

---

1   Argyris, C. (1985) *Action Science, Concepts, Methods, and Skills for Research and Intervention* (San Francisco: Jossey-Bass) provides a useful overview of this. An excellent description of the works of Chris Argyris can be found at <http://www.infed.org/thinkers/argyris.htm>.

boardroom, rather than in public. However, if the message has got out, then it will need correcting, publicly.

If the manager in question has been given a chance to 'get on the bus', and has chosen not to, when the bus is leaving, it is now too late. The alternative is a public execution. By making an example of someone who steps out of line, you also send a clear message about the significance of the strategy to the rest of the organization.

WHEN YOU NEED TO BE SILENT

There are times when you simply cannot communicate the new strategy. You may still be developing the strategy and still require board approval. Or you may be considering options. If these options leak out of the boardroom, then there is a risk that employees may jump to (the wrong) conclusions. Perhaps you have a new product in development, but can't yet tell the sales force when it will be available, as you want them to continue to sell the existing products. Perhaps you are planning to restructure the sales force and significantly change their remuneration. Perhaps you are in a non-disclosure stage of a merger or under financial reporting restrictions.

When approached by an employee and asked a direct question, what do you say? There are three options: say nothing, deny or say that you cannot say anything.

The best solution is often to say nothing so that you avoid starting any rumours. By denying that something is happening, you will be making a clear statement to whomever you are talking to that it is not true, but they may also interpret it as a message that they are not trusted. Saying that you cannot say anything makes a more explicit statement about where you stand in the discussion and that communicating more would be inappropriate.

There are times when an astute employee will realize something is going on and ask you direct questions. As a manager or director, you have a final option: to explain to the employee that it is important that they do not ask such questions, that they should understand the sensitivity of what they are dealing with and that they should respect the commercial sensitivity of the question they are asking. If it is true, then they need to keep quiet about it. If it is not true, then they should not go around talking about it.

WHO TELLS THE STORY OF YOUR STRATEGY?

As a consultant I have a golden rule about communicating the strategy: it is the management team's strategy, and they should tell it to their staff. Never, as an external consultant, get in a position where you are telling it to the organization's staff for the first time. A member of the client's staff should communicate it. They are the ones who will be implementing it and delivering it, not the consultant. The consultant's role is to help them with a successful implementation.

As a consultant, I will happily run through their strategy when playing it back to the management team. At times I may tell the story on a one-to-one basis informally, but it is always to check understanding or just remind people of things they have already seen. It is not to be the messenger of the strategy.

I might spend several hours coaching a director in their presentation skills, content and techniques so they can get the message across well. I may well be sitting watching the audience from the side when they present it. I will help fix any technical problems and be around to manage the process. I will help facilitate discussions and if something needs clarifying I will help. But it is always the client's strategy. They have to believe it, own it, convince others of it, manage it and deliver it.

If you are in marketing, planning or a support role, I would counsel you to take the same approach, unless it is the part of the strategy for your department. As a consultant or facilitator, beware of the danger of slipping into this accidentally during training.

> *Whilst training the top 150 managers in an organization on a new business planning process, the topic of the new business strategy came up. It was clear that this was also a chance to reinforce the messages of the new strategy and how the business planning process supported it. If I had gone ahead on my own, without client support, I would have been telling them, with no authority, to change their practices and would have taken the brunt of any concerns over the new strategy.*
>
> *Instead, I had two people support the session. A senior director introduced the session, emphasizing its importance and the objectives of the session. Now, I was working off his authority. If there were questions of strategy, policy and direction that I could not answer, I could simply refer them back to him.*
>
> *Second, I had a supporting member of client staff from the policy and strategy team on the course supporting me. Not only were they the permanent point of contact for the new business planning process, their role was to both gauge the audience and to provide detailed content in specific areas. They also provided continuity. They were responsible for the maintenance and support of the new business planning process and had the resources to support it.*

Occasionally, you might use a professional to help you get a part of your message across to your customers. Here you are augmenting the management team's message, which is quite different.

A new chief executive officer (CEO) was communicating a turnaround strategy in a large insurance company. He was not a natural presenter. He chose to get assistance in presenting. He employed a serious journalist from the BBC, with a reputation for asking tough questions on current affairs programmes. The journalist was briefed on the changes planned and then let loose in the organization to interview people, get their views, questions and concerns, and prepare a set of questions for the CEO.

The whole of the head office gathered in the central atrium of the building. Centre stage was the new CEO and the journalist who introduced the session and then posed questions he had gathered from the staff to the new CEO.

What was clear was that the new CEO had the answers and answered what he believed. He was not a natural presenter and performer, so he looked a little uncomfortable, but his answers were assured. The effect in terms of getting the message across to several thousand people simultaneously was extremely good.

In this situation, the presenter is not telling the story of the strategy, but acting on behalf of the audience to ask questions about the strategy. They are representing the audience and helping the management team tell the story.

Questions

Who should present the strategy?

How well do they understand and own it?

How well prepared are they?

What do they need to learn to do this well?

Who could help you get the message across?

CONCLUSION

It is vital that, as a management team, you all give out the same message. It is the chief executive's role to ensure that the team is aligned, in the sense of understanding the same things, telling the same story and 'singing from the same hymn sheet'.

Ensuring a high quality conversation has gone on within the boardroom is also vital to this process. When the strategy has been developed by only part of the team, it is necessary to ensure the rest of the team are brought into the group and share the understanding.

Well rehearsed and careful briefing of those around the management team will ensure that a consistent message is passed to the next tier of management. This requires careful checking that the message has been communicated and understood as intended.

There will be a time when this does not happen as effectively as you would like. Sometimes it will require a simple correction of the message, or a simple re-education of the person involved. At other times it may be deliberate miscommunication or disruption. In these cases more radical surgery may be required.

Finally, it is an advantage if you have consultants and other third parties to assist in your strategy, but in the end it is *your* strategy. Your people will judge you and the strategy by the conviction you bring to it. Don't let others tell it for you. Tell it yourself, with consistency and integrity.

9 The Handcuffed Organization

In the last chapter, we explored how an inconsistency of message within the management team will show up as a lack of integrity, congruence or consistency. However, even if the team are giving a consistent message, the organization as a whole can be communicating an inconsistent message, which will make it appear that the whole story lacks integrity.

This lack of integrity is embedded in the organization. There are many processes, activities and practices that support the organization on a day-to-day basis: budgeting, individual performance plans, recruitment, projects and many more. The lack of integrity can come from one or many of these sources. It is important to ensure these are also aligned with the message.

If you fail to do this, you may believe you have the best strategy, that you are communicating it in the most congruent and effective way, but it will fail, because the organization's systems, structures, practices and processes will stop it happening. Failing to address these issues will mean that you effectively handcuff the organization and restrict its ability to execute your strategy.

In this chapter we identify the sources of potential incongruity and provide some suggestions as to what you can do about them. There are five main components of organizational alignment:

- the financial system and budgets;
- investments in programmes and projects;
- individual objective setting, appraisal and rewards;
- recruitment;
- other processes.

Finally, we will consider the timing of changes, as you can't do everything at once, and the messages associated with timing.

THE FINANCIAL SYSTEMS AND BUDGETS

The finance and budgeting systems are extremely influential mechanisms in an organization. Imagine the situation where you are trying to execute the new strategy, but the budgets are still operating under the old strategy. Imagine trying to implement a strategy that the budgets don't even reflect. This sounds unlikely, doesn't it? Yet, research[1] shows that 60 per cent of organizations do not have budgets that reflect their strategy. If this is true, nearly two out of every three organizations may be struggling with a strategy that wants to achieve one thing and a set of budgets that are holding it back.

Usually this inconsistency is not in the area of the main 'programme of change'. Most organizations are careful to fund this. The misalignment occurs where, in 'business as usual', departmental managers are trying to follow the new strategy, but are being constrained by the finance system's processes or the existing budgets.

In some cases the accounting practices discourage common sense. You will have heard of situations where the budget needs to be spent before the end of the financial year. If the budget owners do not spend what is in the budget, then they will get it cut. Their budget is simply calculated on last year's budget plus, say, 4 per cent. The alternative would be to ask what elements made up the budget from scratch and to recalculate (zero-based budgeting). However this takes far more time and many organizations resort to the simpler, but cruder, inflation increases.

This crude approach means that budgeting is not a transparent process. As a consequence, people learn to behave dysfunctionally. They ask for more than they need, expecting to be cut back. Hopefully, if they are skilful enough they will be seen to have given up some, but have kept enough to run their department.

Sales people used to be renowned for a similar trick. They might have sales targets that are raised if they over perform. In good months, sales might be held over in the bottom drawer for the next month. That way their sales target stays more smooth and consistent. They also have some start towards the next target. As they say, 'Always meet the numbers, never beat them.' The opposite is true to the declaration of income in publicly listed organizations. Extreme care needs to be taken over the booking of revenue. In some cases over-optimistic booking has led to the demise of a company.

It may be that the cost codes or the coding structure of the accounts don't permit the investment, or don't allow you to allocate it properly. A problem may occur if the chart of accounts is inflexible or the effort to change proves

---

1   In-house research conducted by Renaissance Worldwide Ltd (1998), 'Barriers to strategy implementation', and others since.

too much. When new organizational structures are introduced, new products areas created or new pay systems introduced, the chart of account lags behind the new structure. Budgets may be prepared for the new organization but the accounting systems may lag behind the change.

It might be that the financial objectives or the targets have changed, but the budget has not. This tends not to be the case with capital budgets, as the capital tends to be allocated from the overall investment programme, though timing differences do occur. However, revenue budgets that support the operational, day-to-day, costs can often get left behind.

This may be because a department is genuinely being asked to do more with less. If that is the case, you need to tell people and make it explicit. Perhaps the strategy is about eliminating unnecessary rules, complexity, hand-offs between people and duplication of checking. Then costs may be reduced at the same time as productivity and service improve.

At other times you may be asking people to take on more things. In some organizational cultures, there seems to be a slow but persistent dribble of more change slowly poured on to departments with the expectation, in each case, that the additional work generated by the change should be absorbed within the existing team's workload and resources.

A city council had a long track record of working in separate silos (see chapter eight on silo thinking). The new strategy started to encourage and develop working between the silos, especially where the departments served the same people in the community. In some cases this meant that it might be appropriate for departmental managers to reallocate some of the budget from one department to another to ensure the best overall service for the community. This 'letting go' of their budgets ran completely counter to their culture, which had been one of holding on to as much budget as possible, keeping their departmental budgets to themselves and squirreling away pots of funds so that they were able to make changes and improvements despite budget restrictions across the council as a whole.

Six months into the change programme, some departments were starting to loosen up and agree areas where there was more appropriate allocations of work, effort and therefore funding. Slowly, the many years of mistrust, hiding of funds and careful (cunning) accounting were starting to unwind.

Then central government introduced a series of cost-cutting programmes across all the councils in the country (The Gershon review). This meant budget cuts were required again. The finance department decided, unilaterally, to request a 10 per cent cut in departmental budgets across the board. They also insisted on them being found in the next 2 months. Up until then, there were budget savings coming out between departments through the more appropriate allocation of resources and effort. The funding was starting to follow the community and resource needs.

The effect was immediate. Departmental managers and directors retreated to their silos and the cost reduction challenge became a lose–lose game: 'If I find savings of 12 per cent that means that you only have to find savings of 8 per cent, and that is not fair. So, it is in my interests to find some savings, but not at the expense of someone else not having to make savings in their departments.' The time for careful thinking had passed. Collaboration stopped. The joined up thinking and working came to an abrupt halt while budgets were protected against arbitrary cuts.

You might be initiating a deliberate cost reduction and 'wake up' exercise, trying to break people out of their existing lethargy, so that they actively look for ways to do things more effectively and efficiently, with fewer people.

When a change programme was launched, the chief executive made it clear there would be 10 per cent budget cuts in every department. Each manager had 2 months to come up with the 10 per cent cuts. It was made clear that the place was operating inefficiently with unnecessary rules, practices and procedures as well as excess spending.

It was also made clear that if the managers did not come up with the 10 per cent saving, then the chief executive would find the 10 per cent for them. So it was also symbolic of their willingness to try and make changes happen and to become a more efficient organization.

The savings proposals were to be brought to the management team and explained to them. There was to be no hiding place and no excuses.

The accounting and budgeting systems are powerful mechanisms of control in organizations. If you leave the accounting practices, structures or budgets in place, they can do a marvellous job of contradicting and undermining your strategy. It is not just capital investments and change programmes that need appropriate funding: the operational budgets need to be tackled as well.

Budgeting and accounting systems also provide a powerful way to communicate change in the organization. They can be used to demonstrate that *even the accounting systems, budgets and practices* are changing. This can be a complementary message to the organization alongside your other announcements.

Questions

Are the budgets, accounting practices and structures supporting your strategy or acting against it?

Have you made appropriate changes to capital budgets and revenue accounts to support the strategy?

Where might you be sending conflicting signals with the accounting systems?

How could you make the change easier to implement? How could you send a clearer and consistent signal, using the budgets and accounting systems?

THE PROJECTS AND PROGRAMMES OF WORK

An organization needs to ensure its programme of investment in change is also aligned with the strategy. If you are not investing in the right projects and areas, or your managers are focusing on projects that support the old strategy, then you will send the wrong message. If you fail to put the resources behind the new strategy, or spread people so thinly that they cannot deliver the projects, you are also likely to fail. On the other hand, if you get the right projects, resources, commitment, ownership and energy behind the right set of projects, you will reinforce your message and are far more likely to succeed.

When a new strategy is being implemented, it is usually accompanied by a programme of change or a collection of projects and initiatives designed to support the strategy. This may or may not include projects that are underway already. It will certainly affect people who are involved with projects that are underway already.

Several things can get in the way of projects being successful. These include:

- existing projects;

- projects not designed to support the strategy;

- project management disciplines;

- ownership and accountability;

- allocation of resources and capacity;

- management of expectations.

It always surprises me how many projects are running in organizations. It often surprises the management team when they see an inventory of how many are actually going on in their organization. This may be because the organization is not running an overall programme management or even project management approach. In most organizations, the project inventory reveals anything between 100–200 projects, though typically I stop around 120 or so, as this is usually reveals sufficient detail. If this sounds a large number, I have found it to be true in organizations as diverse as £20 million manufacturing organizations, local authorities and several billion pound FTSE100 companies. In larger companies, with time and effort, you can easily find this many projects in each of the divisions or regions.

These projects can fall into many categories. They include projects designed to improve compliance and support new regulations in the organization, others to improve operational efficiency, some associated with major change, investments in new product development and investment in the organization's people and their capabilities. They exclude projects that are for the customer, for instance a consultancy or software house delivering a new application for a customer.

This process of collecting the projects together often exposes how much change is going on in the organization. Not all of these are 'strategic' in the sense of supporting the key changes that will differentiate the position of the organization for the future. Many are incremental improvements designed to make the place better on a day-to-day basis.

All these projects are consuming resources, potentially funding and certainly management attention. Some of these resources will be embedded in the departments and absorbed as 'business as usual'. Others will be dedicated to the larger projects. With this many projects in an organization, it is easy to see why some report change fatigue.

Introducing a new programme of change on top of the existing programme may lead to overload and delivery failure. Go through the projects, identify which are still relevant, decide which need cutting and which need some support or realignment.

In a large retailer, there were over 150 projects representing around £100 million of investment. The collection process was the first time these projects had been seen by the board in their entirety. Having collected them in, the management team spent time aligning the projects against the strategy they had developed.

There were some projects that seemed an anachronism and people puzzled why they were even there. There were some projects that were local efficiency improvements, which were up to the local managers to decide whether they would really deliver the goods. Many of these were loosely defined and had poorly constructed benefit cases.

In some cases there were projects that still supported the strategy and were clearly important. Other projects looked as if they should support the strategy, but needed realigning. Some had been conceived some years ago. Others looked as if they were duplicating the work of another project: they could be rationalized.

In the end they concluded that approximately £40 million of the £100 million worth of projects appeared to make no contribution towards the strategy. These were candidates for cost reduction or reallocation of investments and resources.

There are six tests to apply to these projects:

1.   Are they necessary? Do they make a difference to the strategy? If not, why are they there?

2. Are they sufficient? Will these projects be sufficient to bring about the benefits and change that are intended?

3. Are they cost effective? Is the return worth the investment?

4. Are they managed and controlled well enough to ensure delivery?

5. Are they being given the resources and commitment they need?

6. Finally, do we have the resources to deliver all of this across the organization?

These questions act as a filter on projects to ensure that they are actually relevant to the strategy, will deliver, and will deliver cost effectively.

Questions

Do you have projects and investments that are still trying to implement the old strategy?

What projects and investments are needed to make the new strategy happen?

Are you clear about these? Are you able to communicate your objectives and ensure they are aligned with the strategy?

Are they sufficiently funded and resourced?

The discipline of project management

Many organizations use project management methods[2] such as PRINCE2[3] to ensure their staff manage projects well and operate a disciplined approach. These methods are extremely valuable in providing a common language for projects, ensuring standards are met, and giving people the skills and techniques to manage projects. They embody good practices and techniques bundled together in a logical sequence of work, together with appropriate controls and disciplines. They also develop their confidence that they are following an appropriate approach and which steps to follow to ensure the right elements are put in place.

The culture of the organization must also support these trained project managers. Even the best trained and experienced ones will fail in an organization that pays lip service to accountability, sponsorship, providing resources, signing-off specifications and applying disciplined change control.

---

2   These methods are often incorrectly referred to as 'methodologies'. It is a rare case where an -ology is not used for the study of something. This is unfortunate as it detracts from the study of methods and causes people not to study the common features and differences between methods. This is a shame.
3   PRINCE (Projects in Controlled Environments) was first developed by the UK government in 1989 as the standard approach to IT project management for central government. PRINCE2 has been widely adopted and adapted by both the public and private sectors and is now the UK's de facto standard for project management. For more information see <http://www.prince2.org.uk>.

The PRINCE2 approach includes training for project sponsors and those of steering boards. This ensures that they too understand what is required of them as well as what they should require of their project managers. Having the right level and type of sponsorship is a common area of weakness and risk on projects, which leads to poor support for project managers and the projects themselves.

Another element includes appreciating and being sensitive to the level of project management discipline to apply to different sized projects. Many reject these project management disciplines as over-bureaucratic and demanding too much paperwork. This is usually a sign of poorly understood practices, failure to appreciate the benefits that each stage brings to the whole project or trying to apply every procedure and piece of paper to the project, no matter what is really appropriate. Some organizations can make the process too bureaucratic, just as others can be too lax.

Questions

What project and programme management disciplines are in place?

Do you have the project management and sponsorship skills?

Do you support your programme and project managers to deliver the benefits?

What else do they need from you?

Ownership and accountability

Good practice tells us that projects are not owned in support functions such as IT, human resources and finance. They are owned by the main business units and in particular by the directors and managers of those units. There is a simple reason for this. These people are both responsible and accountable for delivering the results and benefits of the projects.

You may meet situations where the projects are not owned by the managers in the areas that are due to implement them. They are being implemented by project managers who may be sitting in, perhaps, IT or a project management function. When the projects are due to be delivered, there is little support from the business unit affected. I call this 'pushing string'.

This is a fundamental problem of accountability and ownership. It is a problem that probably goes right back to the start of the project when the initial business case was conceived, developed and approved. If the managers in the area did not believe the benefits would come, did not want the benefits that were expected, or simply made up some numbers to keep accounting happy, then the project will be a failure.

Sometimes the project managers will be focused on completing a project, despite the limited support from 'the business'.[4] Others may realize that their responsibility is to deliver benefits, not projects. The right thing to do if a project is unsupported and not likely to deliver benefits is to have it stopped, at least until there is appropriate support. It does nobody's career any good delivering projects that will not deliver benefits.

A large accountancy and consultancy firm were implementing a customer relationship management system amongst its partners. It was running this as an internal project with its own development team. However the project had stalled. The software was well underway, but there seemed to be little support amongst the partnership. A new project manager was brought in who quickly assessed the situation.

It became clear very quickly that the issue was not the software that was being developed, but the commitment amongst the partners to use it. The approach relied on the partners inputting their contacts so all could see them, and share them. This improved visibility of the overall relationship with client organizations. From this the relationships could be managed more systematically.

However, the culture of the organization, and particularly the individual partners, was one of, 'these are my clients and my relationships'. It very soon became apparent that the commitment from the partners to input and share their personal black books was not there.

Whereas the previous project manager had hit the same problem, and so focused on the technology, this new project manager concentrated on the relationships and cultural blocks. It soon became clear that the most senior partners with the biggest clout and leverage over the other partners were as much to blame as any of them. As a consequence, the project was stopped, saving the wasted development team costs, until the cultural elements could be resolved properly.

Another situation can occur where there is no accountability for the savings and benefits that are planned. Many examples of this exist where projects are forecast to save costs, perhaps in manpower, but the costs are not removed from the departmental budgets at the appropriate time. The starting point is that either the project has failed or the budgets can be cut.

As the project neared completion, the finance director approached the customer service director. He held the initial project justification in his hands. 'So, we were talking about a 5 per cent reduction in headcount from the new customer service system, an increase in 15 per cent productivity across the rest of the staff and improvements in both staff retention and customer retention. I know we have had some increases in sales volumes which has also increased

---

4   This expression 'the business' is a fallacy, as it suggests the person using it is not in the business, but somewhere else. Of course the project manager is also part of the business.

customer service activity, so lets look at the figures shall we and see what needs adjusting.'

In communicating the strategy, it is vital that this accountability and ownership is highly visible and explicit. This can be through a visible presence on the project or in project boards, expressions of the importance of the project, emphasis of deadlines, allocation of resources or putting highly regarded people on the project. These signs of ownership and commitment are particularly important in organizations where there has been a track record of projects that are not really owned or have limited accountability for their benefits.

Programme and project management

A colleague once described to me the difference between programme management and project management. 'Project management builds houses. Programme management builds communities.' She made an important point. It is the combination of a set of projects that delivers the overall benefits to the organization. It is the timing and integration of effort, resources and deliverables across a set of projects that makes the real difference.

Programmes of work should fit naturally with the ownership of themes of the strategy. One programme might be concentrating on product development, whilst another gets customer service sorted out, or removes costs in the operations areas. This natural organization of projects into programmes makes it easier to place ownership and accountability for a programme in a single place. It also makes the programmes of work easier to manage, resource, integrate and control.

Questions

What are the natural programmes of work for your strategy?

Who are the natural owners of these programmes?

Are they responsible and accountable for the whole programme?

Are they clearly demonstrating their commitment to the strategy?

Managing expectations

The credibility of your communications will be undermined if you set expectations of unrealistic delivery timescales for projects. This will be especially true if the organization has a track record of failed delivery of IT systems, for instance. On the other hand, by demonstrating you are serious about the delivery of answers and results to the parts of the change programme you are running, you will change those expectations.

When he launched the change programme, the chief executive made it clear. He was looking for cost savings from the organization over the next 2 months. If they also identified savings that could be removed within the year that also was acceptable. Undoubtedly there were improvements that could be made to the IT systems. However these would take far longer to implement. He made it clear that for this phase, the focus was on how people work, not what IT system changes could improve things.

This chief executive made it clear that there should be no more prevarication and delays using systems as the excuse. The managers had to make a commitment and find savings from the inefficiencies within their working practices and not pass blame and responsibility elsewhere.

Be extra careful to manage expectations when you are dealing with projects that directly alter the customers' experience. It is necessary in all situations, but with these in particular. If you have previously promised changes and these are yet to filter through, a delayed or dropped project could be a major embarrassment.

When working with a large bank, I was asked to assess a project that was out of control. It was not that there were run-away costs: it was far worse than that. Some sales people had got hold of a prototype of a business advisory system, shown it to some customers and then promised some delivery dates. However, what they had seen was a prototype. It looked very convincing. In fact, it required substantial coding and development as well as a significant amount of information being collected and knowledge being encoded into the system.

It was clear when talking to the sales people that the project had been over sold. The issue was not rescuing the project, but managing the expectations of a major client. Having ascertained what had been promised to the client, it was necessary to understand the actual state of the project. This turned out to be insufficient funding, no developer, no project timescales and no one responsible for delivery. Apart from that, it was great.

Having worked out what was possible and what could be funded, as well as the timescales, the sales team who had made the promises were now brought up to speed with what was possible. Fully armed and prepared, they went to the client to explain the situation and what was actually possible. Fortunately, they were sufficiently well trusted and respected by the client that the promises did not become an issue. The project was put on track and face saved as well as client expectations being managed properly.

In this case, clearly something had gone wrong with communications and expectations. It could have had grave consequences because the client involved was a large multinational and therefore a major account for the bank.

In both these examples, with the chief executive and the well-briefed sales team, when you have the facts and are clear about what is possible, people are happy to accept the situation. My experience is problems occur when people sidestep the situation. Problems occur when people are afraid to say what the real issue is, afraid to say that expectations are unrealistic, or have completely unrealistic expectations themselves. These are dangerous situations that can come about from overenthusiasm. They will undermine the strategy very quickly.

Questions

What expectations are you setting for the projects and programmes?

What time scales are these to deliver in?

What promises have been made about your projects?

Are they still realistic?

Whose expectations need to be managed?

Who needs to manage them?

INDIVIDUAL PERFORMANCE PLANS, OBJECTIVES AND REWARDS

Imagine the situation. You agreed your objectives last December and it's now August, but things have moved on. The new strategy has appeared and you can see how your objectives are changing. Yet you know the system demands that bonuses are based upon agreed objectives. So, what are you going to do?

By next December you will be arguing for a bonus based upon objectives that are out of date. Perhaps they are now ridiculously easy to achieve. Perhaps they are now completely outside your control or influence. Isn't it going to influence your thinking over the next few months? How can you renegotiate your goals? How can you reset them given the change in direction? Should you do the right thing and deliver what is needed, or play the corporate game and look to somehow deliver the out of date ones?

These are questions that people ask themselves when a new strategy is announced. They also ask them throughout the whole year, because the annual performance contract assumes that you can reliably set four of five objectives in January and nothing will change in the subsequent 12 months. Things do change, especially when a new strategy is announced. So people have a choice: deliver the original objectives, renegotiate their objectives, trust the organization to accept that things changed, or accept that things have changed and resign themselves to no bonus.

With a change of strategy, these rules may be completely rewritten depending upon the nature of the contract and the bonus arrangements.

There are two separate components to consider here: the appraisal system which should be designed to give people feedback on their performance, help identify areas where people need to develop their skills and help to target people's careers appropriately; and the objective setting and reward system. In many organizations these are intimately linked. In others they are separate with individual development separate from, perhaps, a corporate bonus arrangement.

Quite different systems may operate in different parts of the organization. Therefore, how the appraisal system and reward systems will influence the message of your strategy may vary with the groups, countries or departments with whom you are dealing.

Questions

Does your strategy affect the targets and bonus arrangements?

Have you made it clear what change there is to annual performance targets and bonuses?

What changes to the appraisal system are needed to align with the strategy?

How is it affecting senior management pay and rewards?

How is it affecting the pay and rewards of the rest of the staff?

THE RECRUITMENT PROCESS

Most people think of the recruitment process as a way of finding out what candidates are like. That is only half the story. It is also a way for candidates to experience the culture of the organization they might choose to join. How an organization behaves during recruitment is a statement about what it is like working there.

For many years, my litmus test for an organization's culture was its recruitment process. What happened to me during the recruitment process was a microcosm of what it would be like working for the organization. All the clues were there.

> *I was once interviewed by a large, well known, consultancy. I met a senior manager who first of all asked me about myself, ran through the interview questions and then asked if I had any questions. So I asked about what he thought it was like working for them. 'Well,' he replied, 'I have this child thing at home, but I don't see it very much.'*

That was it. In a single sentence he had summed up the culture of the organization. They had a reputation for taking young graduates and working them really hard. They also had a reputation for burning them up and many left after 4 to 6 years (unless they got promoted). It was obviously a reflection of how he felt about the organization at the time. It clearly leaked out in the recruitment process.

Needless to say, even though I did not have children at the time, I did not pursue that role any further.

This is an extreme example. There are less extreme, but still representative examples, such as the highly bureaucratic recruitment process that involved having to fill in multiple forms and tests, many seeming to duplicate previous ones, or being kept waiting in reception for 30 minutes for the senior partner who was out to lunch and due to interview me. (He then spent the first 10 minutes of the interview working through his pile of CVs as he tried to establish which of them I was.) I recall the seven stage interview process over 4 separate days, spread out over 8 weeks: by the time an offer came through, I had another job. Or being asked to travel the length of the country for an interview, when the post was at their head office only 10 miles from my house, and not being offered expenses for the trip. Each of these provided an insight into the organization. I am sure you have examples of your own.

Your recruitment process tells people what you are like. The type of people you recruit should be the type of people you are trying to encourage and the values you espouse should show through in the behaviours and approach of the interviewers and the process you operate.

Nordstrom is renowned for its customer service.[5] The recruitment process is designed to ensure that only people who have a commitment to customer service are recruited. Then, no matter what grade they aspire to, every employee is required to work on the shop floor serving customers for a year before taking up a new role.

During this time they are expected to demonstrate a commitment to customer service. More importantly, they are assessed by their peers on the quality of the service they provide to customers. Some realize that the commitment is too much and leave. Others are evaluated by their peers during the period on the shop floor and, if they fail to pass this test, they are asked to leave. Many make it through the process having demonstrated their commitment to the customer service ethos and then move on to other roles in the organization.

This way, Nordstrom ensure that they recruit people with a really strong ethos of service and that those people understand what that means to the company and to themselves.

---

5   This is well documented in Collins, J.C. and Porras, J.I. (1999), *Built to Last: Successful Habits of Visionary Companies*, 2nd edn (London: Random House Business Books).

This company make a clear statement about the recruitment process being aligned to underlying principles and values, as well as the strategy of the organization. It also shows how the strategy is generative: it builds a culture of people who understand and demonstrate that they understand customer service. Similarly, others who cannot reach the standards imposed by their peers leave or are invited to leave.

Get a feel for your own organization by asking people what it was like going through the recruitment process. Do it within a week of the interview (whether they joined or chose not to). It will give you great insights in to how the organization projects itself.

Alternatively, apply for a job anonymously.

Make sure you include relationships with any agencies you employ. They experience your processes. They are also reflecting your culture and acting as your ambassadors. It would be a shame if their style contradicted the one that you were trying to project.

Questions

What is your recruitment process like? What signals does it send out?

Does it reflect the sort of people you want to recruit?

What could you do to encourage more of the right people to apply?

What could you do to encourage more of the right people to select you through the process?

OTHER PROCESSES

This does not just apply to recruitment. It applies just as well to the organization's other processes.

Imagine working with an organization that really cares about innovation and research. Their raw material needs to have excellent properties and be constantly updated and refreshed. Their raw material list changes every 3 years. Then consider the 'corporate rottweiler' they have employed in procurement, who actively drives prices down with suppliers and pays no attention to the relationship or to product quality. Despite their potential for collaboration and partnership on innovation, the more innovative organizations walk away because they cannot afford to offer an innovative service at rock bottom prices, compared with suppliers who do not attempt to innovate. Purchasing is destroying the innovation in the process.

Imagine a call centre in a charity.[6] The people joined the charity because they care about the cause as well as the job. Then imagine a call centre system that is undercapacity, so that callers are on the line for up to 20 minutes trying to get through. By the time they do get through the callers are angry and annoyed. They take it out on the call centre staff. As a result, these call centre staff don't stay very long. It is not a highly paid job anyway. They want to feel they are making a difference, yet end up being harangued when a caller gets through. It is no surprise that there is a high turnover of call centre staff.

Imagine an organization where its IT systems do not support its needs. You are trying to treat customers as individuals, but your separate IT systems have inconsistent information about the same person on them. Perhaps its website claims it offers customer service yet its systems make it difficult to buy or contact an individual when you need to talk to one. There are many examples like these, where the organization and its internally or externally facing systems hold back or contradict the message it is trying to put across.

These are simple examples of where the message sent out by the process is contradictory to the message that the organization wants to send out. In these cases it causes frustration and has the effect of handcuffing the organization and constraining the strategy.

Questions

Are there parts of your organization where the processes are contradicting the strategy?

What processes and procedures do you need to think about that should support the strategy?

Do they support the strategy (or do they work against it)?

What could you do to improve this alignment?

A CULTURE OF HANDCUFFED PEOPLE

The underlying reasons for these handcuffed processes, systems, practices and behaviours can be deeply embedded in the psyche of the organization and may have their origins in its history.

This is illustrated by a rather sad experiment on gorilla behaviour that illustrates this point. As you read this, bear in mind I don't condone this experiment. I hope it is just a story. Though I'm sure you will recognize the implications for your organization.

6　This example is from the TV series, *Back to the Floor*, where Peter Davies, the director general of the RSPCA, visited one of the charity's call centres in Manchester (BBC2, series 2, episode 4, originally broadcast 1 December 1998).

The Gorillas and the Bananas.

A group of seven gorillas are in a cage. They like bananas. When bananas were lowered into the cage they would grab them. The experimenters would squirt the gorillas with cold water when they went for the bananas. Moreover, when any one of the group went for a banana they all got soaked. Guess what? After a while the gorillas stopped going for the bananas.

Then they swapped one gorilla out and put another one in. As the banana was lowered in the new one went for it and it and all the rest got soaked. Very soon it learnt not to go for bananas.

Another was swapped out. This time when the bananas were lowered in, the existing gorillas grabbed the new gorilla before it could get to the banana and get them all soaked. Now the new gorilla didn't know why. He just got mugged every time the bananas appeared.

Another gorilla is swapped out and the same thing happens again. They kept doing this until there were none of the original gorillas. The hosepipe was not used again. Yet when a new one came in, they would get mugged when the bananas were lowered in – and never know why. They just continued the tradition.[7]

The moral of this story is fairly clear.

TIMING

One aspect common to all of these is timing. How do you ensure consistency across these various processes and messages, when there is a lot of work to change the processes and patterns of behaviour in an organization?

For example, you might change the message of the strategy, but if the annual performance planning, appraisals and bonus setting changes do not coincide with the roll out of the new strategy, then they will be out of alignment.

Where you know these inconsistencies will occur for a while, make them known. Or rather, make it known that you know they are known. The people who are affected by the process will know there are inconsistencies. By signalling that you are aware of them and will compensate for them, you are acknowledging that inconsistencies and incongruities need to be put right. You are also sending a message that a workaround may be acceptable in the interim.

7   I first heard this story associated with a book on lean marketing that refers to the story in its title: Jenkins, D. and Gregory, J. (2003), *The Gorillas Want Bananas* (Great Yarmouth: Bookshaker).

Questions

What are you able to change now?

What will you have to leave until later?

What compromises does this mean? How can you overcome them temporarily?

CONCLUSION

This chapter was called 'the handcuffed organization' because the mechanisms, processes and characteristics of the organizations can act to handcuff the people you are trying to change. They may want to help you, but will be unable to unlock these handcuffs themselves.

A variety of mechanisms can handcuff the strategy: IT systems, accounting systems, recruitment processes, the appraisal system. Often these are deeply embedded in the organization, like the accounting structures, attitudes to project ownership or recruitment processes. Often these are so much part of the psyche of the organization that people do not even realize that they are things that can be changed: 'It is how we have always done it.'

If you communicate the message of the new strategy, and fail to realize that these handcuffs exist, people will think you are not serious, and the message will lack congruity. You will be trying to communicate the enthusiasm of the strategy, only to have people say, 'That will never happen here.' You might be thinking things are moving along, only to accidentally leave road blocks in the way. You may not realize these are impediments and handcuffs exist until things start to slow in the treacle of change. Your role will often be to set an example or give permission for these handcuffs to be broken, as has been demonstrated in previous chapters. If you can anticipate these and fix them beforehand, then the changes to these deeply embedded practices will also act as important signals that communicate your intention to deliver the strategy.

10 Developing Your Communications Strategy and Plan

This chapter brings together all the advice, ideas and elements into the overall communications plan that is implemented with the strategy.

Some of the advice and content transcends the stages of the strategy. Chapter seven, for instance, provides techniques for telling the story of the strategy that can be applied at each and every stage of the strategy planning, design and implementation process. Other chapters will have more relevance to particular stages of the process. This chapter puts all the topics into the context of a strategy being designed, communicated and implemented.

When strategy is planned, designed and implemented it tends to go through a number of stages. There are many variations on these.[1] However, for our purposes we can break the process into five stages. These are:

        Stage 1: Strategic analysis and planning

        Stage 2: Strategic design and implementation planning

        Stage 3: Launching the strategy

        Stage 4: Follow-up and commitment

        Stage 5: Embedding the strategy and tracking results.

Let's take these stages in turn and relate the most relevant chapters to them.

STAGE 1: STRATEGIC ANALYSIS AND PLANNING

Strategic analysis usually involves detailed research into the market, consumers and customers, competition, and other factors in the external environment that will influence and affect the strategy. Strategic planning

---

1   For a description of the different schools of strategy and how they address the strategy planning process differently, see Mintzberg, H, Ahlstrand, B. and Lampel, J.B. (1998), *Strategy Safari: A Guided Tour through the Wilds of Strategic Management* (Harlow: Pearson Education).

involves choices about what the organization wants to achieve and which strategy is best suited to achieve it.

Consequently, most of the activity during this phase will be within the boardroom, amongst the directors or between the team involved in strategic planning and the executive.

Two chapters are particularly useful during this stage. Chapter six provides advice that acts as a checklist for the breadth of discussions. It includes the creation of a mission statement that also contains a compelling future, which is made as tangible as possible so those involved have the richest understanding of how each other thinks the future will develop. It includes having clear targets. It emphasises how the strategy needs to provide a clear path to the future, including cause and effect, avoiding strategy by hope and magic, and recognizing the tensions and contradictions that all strategies contain.

Chapter eight moves the emphasis from the content of the strategy to the quality of the discussion and thinking about the strategy amongst the management team. When the discussion ensures a deep understanding of the elements of the strategy, amongst the team, there is a far greater likelihood that everyone will leave the boardroom telling the same story. How these discussions are managed during this stage of the strategy development will have a critical impact on the quality of alignment amongst the team once the strategy is spread beyond the board room.

STAGE 2: STRATEGIC DESIGN AND IMPLEMENTATION PLANNING

Once a strategy has been chosen from amongst the various options available, the next step is to detail the strategy, design how it will be implemented and plan that implementation.

The story of the strategy can be further developed in this stage, using the techniques from chapter six in more detail. At the same time, as strategy is invariably about change, chapter four provides useful tools to think about how the change will be managed. When the past has become unacceptable, or tough decisions are to be made, this stage is usually where that message is planned for later delivery. As well as the various mechanisms of change, the overall change model can be used as a framework to assist in the strategic design and planning process.

Chapter 9 looks at the handcuffed organization and asks whether there are processes, practices, beliefs, or other elements of the organization's behaviours that would hold back the implementation of the strategy. These should be addressed during this strategy implementation stage. By the end of this stage you should have a clear programme of projects and investments that support your strategy. You should also be clear about the resources necessary to implement the strategy. Finally, you will have a plan for eliminating those elements that will act against the strategy and delay or undermine its success.

Whilst the details of the strategy are being developed, the plans for launching and communicating the strategy should also be developed. Chapters 3, 4 and 5 provide ideas to think through the stakeholders and players involved, the channels to communicate with them, and how they may receive the message.

Ensure that you make sufficient time for this stage. Designing the strategy often takes longer than expected. When timescales for launching the strategy are fixed, the item that gets squeezed is the communication planning. The more the communication and planning elements and team members are integrated into the same team, the easier this stage becomes.

STAGE 3: LAUNCHING THE STRATEGY

Before the strategy is launched, you should have a clear plan for the next 2 to 3 months of communication. What will be communicated, when, by whom and at which events? At the same time you should have briefed, prepared and rehearsed the individuals who will deliver the message.

In larger organizations, the 'launching the strategy' phase is often allocated between 1 and 2 months. During this time the messages are clearly communicated to the staff and other players involved. Any hard messages are sent out and any fallout from the message handled. This short period acts as an initial review milestone for the strategy communication project.

During this stage, people will be asked to understand that 'the platform is burning', or that 'the bus is preparing to leave'. They may be asked to make decisions about showing commitment and supporting the strategy. Some may choose not to make the journey.

Any external investor and statutory communication will also occur at this stage. You will be setting their expectations at this stage and continuing to manage them as the strategy gets rolled out.

Your team should have regular reviews of progress during this stage. Hold them at least weekly, with more major reviews monthly. Make sure you know how the communication is working and check up on the feedback you are receiving. If you have asked for a commitment to change and action by, say, 2 months, ensure that this is followed up.

During this stage your key managers and directors will be using the communications skills they already have or have developed using the advice in Chapters 6 and 7.

STAGE 4: FOLLOW-UP AND COMMITMENT

After the initial launch period of 1 to 2 months, you should expect to see the changes coming through. Set another period of no more that 3 months during which you will reinforce the message, expect to see lasting commitment and be implementing the other projects and measures that are a part of your strategy.

You may have to refine and elaborate the story of the strategy as it develops during this phase. Ensure that these messages also emerge through the channels as efficiently as the first messages.

During this phase, you may be spending more time with external partners such as customers or suppliers. You may have informed them already of the changes and they should have noticed some changes starting to happen. This is a chance to involve them in the process as well.

You should also be hearing success stories by now. Publicize these as examples of what you are trying to achieve. They will not only reinforce your story, but will act as morale support and signs that you are making real progress.

STAGE 5: EMBEDDING THE STRATEGY AND TRACKING RESULTS

Strategy design and implementation is a continuous process. After the initial period of 3 to 6 months, you should see the changes being embedded within the organization. You should also start to see the tangible results coming through from the behavioural changes you have encouraged.

You should still continue to communicate the strategy and results with external investors, suppliers and customers, as well as your staff.

You should also be refining your message as you learn from the implementation of the strategy and refine the strategy itself.

CONCLUSION

This chapter brings together the contents of the previous chapters into a typical strategy implementation timetable. The timescale is only indicative and you should choose for yourself how fast you believe you can implement your strategy and communicate it effectively. However, these stages and timescales provide a framework in which you can plan your strategy's communication.

11 Final Thoughts

As this book was being written, we are seeing a large increase in social networking and collaboration over the Internet. Sites such as MySpace, YouTube, eBay, linkedin, among many others, are providing people with the chance to both link to others with similar affiliations and share information. A key element of these sites is the development of trust among the participants.

At the same time many organizations are using these sites to create viral marketing opportunities, post snippets from television programmes, let out fun videos with a corporate placement in them and generally get their message out. In the past, disgruntled employees and company leavers vented their feelings in discussion groups such as Yahoo and other places. Hopefully you will not find your corporate strategy for sale on eBay, your company strategy video on MySpace or your employees openly burning your company mission statement on YouTube. It is probably already happening, right now, to someone.[1]

In the same way as these sites develop trust and affiliation, you have the challenge of developing trust amongst your employees and staff. If you leave it that only a small percentage understand the strategy, or you communicate it in a way that does not develop trust and integrity, then a leading indicator will be the public embarrassment of publication on a social networking site.

On the other hand, by treating your employees with respect, trusting them, helping them understand your thinking so they can contribute to your strategy, you have a far higher chance of succeeding.

---

1   It took me only 2 minutes on YouTube to find an example of a company mission statement being burnt, simply by putting different company names into the site's search engine.

APPENDIX
The Channels: Communicating the Message

This book has referred to a variety of communication channels. This appendix summarizes the characteristics and relative effectiveness of the various channels you might use.

169

For each channel the tables summarize:

- Whether the channel reaches a broad audience or is more narrow and personal

- Whether the channel provides feedback

- The reliability of the channel

- Its ability to carry a rich message

- The time to prepare a message for the channel

- The speed of communication through the channel

The channels are divided into three groups:

Table A.1 Summary of the Effectiveness of Various Face-to-Face Communication Channels

Table A.2 Summary of the Effectiveness of Various Electronic and Internet Based Communication Channels

Table A.3 Summary of the Effectiveness of Other Communication Channels

Channel	Description and example	Broad or narrow; personal or impersonal	Feedback: one way or two way?	Reliability	Ability to get a rich message across	Time to prepare	Speed of communication
One-to-one (face-to-face) management meetings	Individual face-to-face briefings and meetings. (For example, individual goal-setting or redundancy meetings.)	Very personal. Delivers individual messages very well.	Provides immediate feedback. Amount received depends on style.	Very reliable. Critically dependent on person giving the message.	Permits a rich message. Necessary to ensure the simple message is also communicated.	General message may have to be prepared on a one-to-one basis.	Slow, as everyone has an individual meeting.
Team cascade briefings	Uses existing team meetings. Cascade through them as a structured briefing.	Gets a broadcast out through a narrow channel very quickly.	Provides immediate feedback from discussions in relatively small groups.	Highly reliable. Relies on quality of management briefing.	High quality, face-to-face communication. Can be supported with other media.	Worth spending time preparing managers and rehearsing tough questions. Several weeks.	Once started, very quick and effective.
Company conferences	Large company conferences.	Tends to be broadcast, with limited small group interaction.	Mainly one way. Breakout groups give some limited two-way feedback.	Moderately to highly reliable. Limitation is in the feedback.	Tends to be presentations, though improves when also includes other methods.	Takes substantial time and organization, 3 to 4 months at least, especially booking venues.	Very effective once underway. Delay in organizing it.

Company gatherings	Monthly gathering of whole factory or department in common area (for example, in the canteen).	Broad and relatively personal.	People get a chance to ask questions and give feedback.	Very reliable. Good way to get and reinforce a message.	Good. Can use presentations, talks, videos as necessary.	Preparation required, and rehearsal advised. Can be delivered at short notice.	Can be called at short notice.
Informal and social networks	Communications amongst informal groups of people (and the rumour mill).	Tend to be multiple one-to-one interactions.	Good at the first level. But you are never quite sure what is being said one step on.	Useful for picking up gossip. Unreliable way of disseminating information.	Good for a rich message, at the first level.	Very short.	Relies on the quality of connections between people.
Workshops	Get a small group or team together on a specific topic, usually facilitated.	Good to get a team.	Can be used for team input and developing understanding amongst a team.	Very reliable, if well prepared.	Provides time to get a rich message across and gather rich feedback.	May need 1 to 2 weeks' preparation, depending on approach.	Can work relatively quickly. Depends upon set-up time and availability.
Management away day	Management team go off to hotel for 2 days to review and discuss strategy.	Good for group discussions bearing in mind only one can speak at a time.	Useful for two-way discussions if facilitated well.	Good way to get alignment, again if facilitated well.	Very good. Can mix presentations, discussions, and other media.	Needs 2 weeks minimum or so notice. Ideally more to prepare people.	Once started, very quick and effective

Table A.1   Summary of the effectiveness of various face-to-face communication channels

Channel	Description and example	Broad or narrow; personal or impersonal	Feedback: one way or two way?	Reliability	Ability to get a rich message across	Time to prepare	Speed of communication
Phone	Personal call.	Personal.	Highly interactive and two-way.	Highly reliable. Not quite as good as face-to-face.	Good, except for pictures, unless used in conjunction with previously sent or shared document.	None.	Very fast on a one-to-one basis.
Email	Bulk email announcements from management team.	One-to-one or one to many.	Good for feedback, though limited by what people are willing to write. You can't see their reaction.	Pretty reliable. Assumes people pick up emails and read them amongst the many in their in-box. Can confirm receipt.	Can add attachments and voice or point to other sources. Good for a thought through statement.	Can be done in a few minutes, assuming distribution lists are in place.	Fast, assuming they pick it up.
Video conference	High bandwidth group video conference in purpose designed room, or one-to-one over the Internet.	Good for one-to-one and small groups. Good to get a single face in front of many people.	Good. Though as size of group increases, distance from camera limits individual feedback.	Very reliable, depending on quality of technology. Building skills with use helps.	Good. Even better when combined with other electronic aids such as shared presentations.	Needs set-up time for equipment.	Very quick. As if face-to-face. Quicker than travelling there.
Text messages	SMS messages on mobile phones used one-to-one or one to many.	Can be one-to-one or one to many.	One to many: limited feedback. One-to-one: limited by constraints of typing.	Assumes person receives message and has phone switched on. No guaranteed delivery.	Very limited.	Short, assuming you have their mobile numbers.	Fast, if they pick it up.
Instant messaging	MSN and AOL instant messaging systems.	Personal. But you probably have not got the person's undivided attention.	Feedback is slow and all has to be types. Emoticons no substitute for hearing and seeing someone.	Reliable in that people see your typed message and can respond.	Limited. Far better to pick up the phone.	None, assuming availability of other person.	Slow to communicate, having to type each line of conversation.

Blogs	Chief executive blogs on their views of the change programme.	Broadcast, not one-to-one.	Mainly one way, though responses allow feedback. Feedback is also public (and may remain so).	Assumes people will know it has been posted, go to it and read it.	Seems more informal than email. Overall picture can emerge from a blog.	Can be produced easily. Write in haste – repent at leisure. Needs regular updates to encourage readers.	Quick to write, but unless blog is fed to people, they only read it when they choose to.
Voice mail	Leaving group or mass voice mail message on the phone system.	Group or mass. More suitable for select groups.	No feedback. Somewhat impersonal.	Assumes people pick up voice messages	Limited to voice.	Needs careful rehearsal and preparation,	Quick.
Electronic newsletters	Weekly or monthly newsletter fed to people on subscription list or posted on intranet.	Broadcast and impersonal. General communication.	One way: sometimes request feedback, but not a reliable channel.	Good for consistency of a prepared message. Can often appear bland.	Reasonable, but limited by scope of newsletter. Often seem to be a restricted format.	Takes time to format well and edit stories and message.	Once out, relies on people knowing it is there and reading it.
Message boards and chat rooms	Discussion forums.	Tends to be impersonal, unless well-developed relationship built up with other correspondents.	Get moderate one-to-one feedback off a few. Not sure who or how many are reading it.	Low. Never know how many are reading it apart from the few that respond.	Very limited.	Quick to do. Relies on people being on the chat room or message board.	Slow. Not sure when read. Posted responses could be any time after.
Webinars (web-seminars)	Web-based presentations, includes interactive PowerPoint presentations and separate voice-overs.	Good for groups from two to three, through to potentially hundreds.	Mainly a presentation, though allows group questions and interaction (usually controlled by moderator).	Very reliable way to get message out (assuming people are paying attention on the other end).	Can get pictures, presentation and words across well. Hard to tell immediate reaction of listeners.	Takes time to prepare presentation, set up webinar and ensure availability.	Good, assuming people are on line and listening. Can be recorded for later review.

Table A.2   Summary of the effectiveness of various electronic and Internet-based communication channels

Channel	Description and example	Broad or narrow; personal or impersonal	Feedback: one way or two way?	Reliability	Ability to get a rich message across	Time to prepare	Speed of communication
Company newspapers	Weekly or monthly physical newsletter. Given out or people can collect them.	Broadcast and impersonal. General communication.	One way: sometimes request feedback, not a reliable channel.	OK for consistency of a prepared message. Can often appear bland.	Reasonable, but limited by media. Often seem to be a restricted format.	Takes time to prepare, edit, print and distribute. Not as quick as electronic versions.	Once out, relies on people knowing it is there and reading it.
Notice boards	Postings on company notice boards, next to the coffee machine.	Scatter gun broadcast. Very impersonal.	One way.	Assumes people will read them. No idea who is reading it. Good for 'for sale' ads.	Can put up presentations.	Easy to put up a notice.	Slow. When people go past and notice it or bother to read it.
Letters home	Used to get a consistent message to a distributed or travelling workforce or team.	Narrow cast to named recipients.	One way. Exception is where a response is required (for example, a survey or form filling in).	Reliable delivery. Unreliable reading.	Envelope could contain anything paper based or CDs. Will it get read though?	Letters need writing, customizing and enveloping. Volume dependent.	Depends upon postal service.
Company video/CD	Presentation from chief executive setting out the issues and what is being done.	Broadcast.	One way, though arranged presentations could be facilitated to gather feedback.	Reliable message. Less reliable on feedback.	Can get very rich message across (for example, interviews with customers and staff, product demos and so on).	Takes time to do well. Anything from 4 to 6 weeks for a good one.	Can be distributed quickly using Internet. Depends on arrangements to be watched.
PowerPoint presentations: presenter there	Group presentation to investors or staff.	Can be used one-to-one or one to many.	Good, assuming presenter allows time for and encourages questions and feedback.	Fairly high. Effective way to get a message across.	Can get pictures, words and emotions across if presented well.	Can be short, depending on skills of person preparing material.	Fast, assuming people are available for the presentation.
PowerPoint presentations: absent presenter	Presentation to investors or staff left on company website	Can be used one-to-one or one to many.	Feedback very limited if presenter is absent.	Limited. Relies on interpretation of slides.	Can get pictures and words across, but not as well as if presented. Very limited emotional impact.	Can be short, depending on skills of person preparing material.	Depends upon people finding it.

Table A.3   Summary of the Effectiveness of Other Communication Channels

Index

If you have found this book useful you may be interested in other titles from Gower

The CEO: Chief Engagement Officer
Turning Hierarchy Upside Down to Drive Performance
John Smythe

978-0-566-08561-1

Grass Roots Leaders
The BrainSmart Revolution in Business
Tony Buzan, Tony Dottino Richard Israel

978-0-566-08802-5

How to Manage a Successful Press Conference
Ralf Leinemann and Elena Baikaltseva

978-0-566-08727-1

Making Knowledge Visible
Communicating Knowledge Through Information Products
Elizabeth Orna

978-0-566-08562-8 (Hardback)

978-0-566-08563-5 (Paperback)

Making the Connections
Using Internal Communication to Turn Strategy into Action, 2nd Edition
Bill Quirke

978-0-566-08780-6

For further information on these and all our titles visit our website – www.gowerpub.com
All online orders receive a discount

GOWER